I0889960

Transforming Negative Self-Talk

Transforming Negative Self-Talk

Practical, Effective Exercises

Steve Andreas

W. W. Norton & Company
New York • London

Copyright © 2012 by Steve Andreas

All rights reserved
Printed in the United States of America
First Edition

For information about permission to reproduce selections from this book, write to Permissions, W. W. Norton & Company, Inc., 500 Fifth Avenue, New York, NY 10110

For information about special discounts for bulk purchases, please contact W. W. Norton, Special Sales at specialsales@wwnorton.com or 800-233-4830

Manufacturing by RR Donnelley Willard
Book design by Ken Gross Production
manager: Leeann Graham

Library of Congress Cataloging-in-Publication Data

Andreas, Steve.
Transforming negative self-talk : practical, effective exercises / Steve Andreas. — 1st ed.
p. cm.
Includes bibliographical references and index.
ISBN 978-0-393-70789-2 (pbk.)
1. Self-talk. 2. Negativism. 3. Criticism, Personal. I. Title.

BF697.5.S47A53 2012
158.1—dc23 2012000107

ISBN: 978-0-393-70789-2 (pbk.)

W. W. Norton & Company, Inc., 500 Fifth Avenue, New York, NY 10110
www.wwnorton.com

W. W. Norton & Company Ltd., Castle House, 75/76 Wells Street, London W1T 3QT

3 4 5 6 7 8 9 0

Contents

Your task is that of altering, not abolishing.

—Milton H. Erickson (in Rossi & Ryan, 1986)

Acknowledgments

> I recall an old Sufi story of a good man who was granted one wish by God. The man said he would like to go about doing good without knowing about it. God granted his wish. And then God decided that it was such a good idea, he would grant that wish to all human beings. And so it has been to this day.
>
> — Robert Fulghum, *All I Really Need to Know I Learned in Kindergarten* (1986)

Through over a half-century of working to understand human nature, and searching for ways that people can improve their lives, I have been influenced by hundreds of thousands. When I think of all the psychologists and therapists who were famous and influential when I was in graduate school in the 1950s, the work of most of them now rests securely in the dustbin of history. However, the work of two stand out as having withstood the acid test of time and results. In my view, Milton Erickson and Virgina Satir were the two greatest therapists who ever lived. However amazing their work was, they were not as adept at transmitting their skills and understandings to their students. Fortunately, they both left behind rich legacies in the form of videos and writings, gold mines for future generations to explore and develop further.

Richard Bandler and John Grinder, the developers of Neuro-Linguistic Programming (NLP) taught me the tools to understand many of the systematic subtleties in how Erickson and Satir worked their magic with suffering people, and I continue to use these understandings to learn and develop yet more and better methods, and make these available to others.

My many thoughtful colleagues—especially my wife Connirae—and participants in training seminars have also contributed immensely by offering me their experience, thoughts, suggestions, and criticism, helping me test and develop better methods and understandings, separating the wheat from the chaff (and in the field of psychotherapy there is an incredible amount of chaff).

Then there are all the others who offered an example, a story, an objection, a question, an observation, or a chance word. Who could notice or remember all the seeds that were planted, and what grew and blossomed from what seemed at the time to be an inconsequential remark? I thank you all for being a part of my life; I hope I have also been, in some small measure, a useful part of yours.

— Steve Andreas

Transforming Negative Self-Talk

Introduction

Nearly everyone has negative internal self-talk at times; some of us have this internal chatter going on almost all the time. An internal voice may remind us of past failures, sorrows, or disappointments, torture us with criticism or verbal abuse, describe frightening or unpleasant futures, or disturb us in other ways. "You failed miserably." "What a loser I am." "I'll never succeed." "Life is a crock." "My life is over." Typically this kind of internal voice causes unpleasant feelings, which are not very helpful in reaching goals and succeeding in life.

A thought like "Nothing I can do will make a difference" in a low, slow voice can easily result in depression. "I'm think I'm about to die" in a rapid, high-pitched tempo can result in anxiety or panic. "Those bastards are out to get me," in a low angry tone can result in violence or paranoia. Often someone's unpleasant feelings are so strong that he or she doesn't realize that they are a response to what an internal voice is saying.

You can probably easily think of sometime in your life when an internal voice did something like this, putting you into an unpleasant state. These bad feelings can be the root cause of a very wide variety of problems, some of them quite serious and long term. In this book I am going to show how these inner voices can be transformed, and how that can make a positive impact in many areas of our lives.

Negative self-talk is something that is not usually under our conscious control; it just happens by itself, and most people find it impossible to stop it or not do it. In fact, trying to stop it generally makes it even more intrusive and troublesome. Our conscious minds are very good at solving many of our problems, but when that fails, we need to learn more about how we function automatically and unconsciously in order to find solutions.

When I use the word *unconscious*, I don't mean Freud's idea of a seething cauldron of forbidden desires; much of our unconscious functioning works very nicely and efficiently, such as when we think to ourselves, "What is his name?" and the name pops into our awareness. I just mean all the aspects of our lives that we don't notice and that we are literally not conscious of. Many of these aspects can become conscious if we pay close attention and ask the right kind of question. That makes it possible to make changes in the process, and then allow the process to be unconscious again.

All of Us "Hear Voices"

The realization that everyone hears internal voices is relatively recent. Not so long ago, most psychiatrists thought that hearing voices was a sign of psychosis, and a few still do. A patient would report hearing voices, and the psychiatrist would say to himself internally, "Hmm, this guy is hearing voices; he must be nuts," without realizing that he was also hearing a voice, and without—in most cases—being nuts himself.

The inner voices of some psychotic patients may sound much louder than what the rest of us hear, and sometimes they may seem to be coming from their surroundings, but it is the same process. In earlier times, hearing an internal voice was thought to be a message from God, the devil, or some other external entity. Even today, some people who commit crimes say that they were ordered to do it by a voice that they heard. "The devil made me do it."

The Benefits of Internal Self-Talk

Hearing internal voices is a natural part of being able to understand and produce language. With the exception of a few people with damage to the language area of the brain, or people who were born completely deaf, we all have internal voices, and usually they provide very useful information and direction. These voices may orient us to tasks that we need to accomplish, alert us to some kind of danger, review the events of the day, and so on. "There's an important meeting tomorrow morning." "Let's get out of here before trouble starts." "I got quite a lot done this week."

Sometimes inner voices offer us useful advice. "Look both ways before crossing a street," is a voice that most parents deliberately try to instill in their small children to protect them from being run over. At other times, an internal voice may simply offer information that is needed to solve a problem, or direct our attention back to an unfinished task. "I wonder if those towels are in the laundry." "I'd better get going on that homework if I'm going to get enough sleep tonight."

My own internal voice has been an essential ally in writing this book. Sometimes I have thought to myself, "There's something missing here." "If this is true, then that must also be true." "How can I say this better?" "That's not very clear; how does that really work?" And there have also been delightful moments of discovery. "Oh, I know how that works!" "I see how these two elements relate to each other!"

Self-Talk Starts Early

Infants begin to learn language by listening to parents and other people around them. The first step in this learning process is to remember the sounds that they heard and to slowly begin to recognize repetitions of those sounds and patterns of sounds. As they are doing this, they are also learning to produce sounds, first by babbling, and then gradually adjusting that babbling to approximate the sounds of the language that they are exposed to. Initially both the sounds that they hear and the sounds that they are learning to produce have no meaning. They are just learning to recognize and produce the sounds of their native language.

The child's next task is to divide the flow of language into separate words, and then to understand what the words mean by connecting them with recurring events. Just as in learning a foreign language, we begin to understand the meaning of what someone else is saying long before we are able to put words together into a reply. These internal voices that we remember are the basis for learning how to produce language and communicate with others around us.

Much later we learn to recognize written words so that we can translate little black squiggles on pages into the sounds of language, and understand books like the one you are reading now. If we had no internal voices, we would not be able to understand the words that others say to us, and we would not be able to communicate with words. We would be forever limited to the nonverbal noises, gestures, and movements that we used as infants.

Words Also Have Music

As we learned the particular words and grammar of the language of our parents, caretakers, or others around us, we also learned all the nonverbal musical sounds of their language—the volume, tempo, rhythm, timbre, intonation, hesitation, regional accent, emotional inflection, and so on.

For instance, when you hear the voice of a stranger, you can determine with close to 100% accuracy if the person is male or female, using these tonal cues—even though you may have no idea what aspects of tonality you are using to do it. And when you answer the phone, usually you can identify who it is by the tonality after hearing only a few words.

Pause right now to remember and listen internally to the voices of several people you know. Recall them one at a time, and hear the distinct tonality that each one uses. First recall the voice of one of your parents, or some other childhood caretaker, such as a grandparent or uncle. . . .

Now hear the voice of another parent or caretaker. . . . *

And then recall the voices of several other important people in your past. . . .

And then some good friends of yours in the present. . . .

Notice how each voice has a distinct tonality. Unless you are musically trained, it might be very hard for you to describe exactly how those voices differ, but you can still hear the differences

* Three dots [. . .] indicates a pause for you to actually do the action described, and discover what you experience. You will only learn fully from this book if you pause for a few moments to try each little experiment.

clearly. Now listen to each voice that you just heard, in turn, and notice how your feelings change in response to each voice. . . .

Those feelings are partly in response to the words that you heard. But they are also in response to the unique tonality of each voice, and to the experiences that you associate with each of those people.

If we were fortunate, our parents were usually kind, nurturing, and understanding, and through imitation we learned to have inner voices that sound that way.

If we were less lucky, our parents may have been angry or even abusive, and we may have learned to talk to ourselves in a tone that is usually critical, distant, gloomy, or dismissive.

And since even the most wonderful parents are sometimes tired, frustrated, irritable, limited, or out of choices, all of us also have memories of times when our parents communicated in ways that were less than ideal. Since this often occurred in situations that stirred strong emotions in us, these may have become strong imprint experiences that affect us throughout our later life—even when most of the time our parents spoke in more caring and reasonable ways.

Every other book on negative self-talk I have seen focuses primarily on the words that we say to ourselves, seldom on the tonality. Yet the tonality of a voice is often a major factor in how we respond to it. For instance, imagine hearing a harsh, sarcastic voice that says, "I love you!" . . .

Then hear a soft, loving, sexy voice saying, "You son of a bitch." . . .

Did you respond primarily to the words or the tonality? When you change the tonality of a troublesome voice, often you don't have to change the words at all in order to change your response. This is one of the aspects of a voice that I will be exploring in great detail.

Most books about negative self-talk are almost entirely devoted to discussing the problems it causes, mistakenly assuming that this kind of "insight" will provide a path to change. In contrast, this book is almost entirely devoted to solutions—what actually works to change the impact of a troublesome voice. Simple exercises and experiments offer opportunities for you to experience ways of changing a voice and to discover what works best for you.

What *Doesn't* Work for Transforming Negative Self-Talk

Someone who experiences a lot of negative self-talk is often willing to do almost anything to quiet the voice and avoid the bad feelings that the voice produces. Many people do this by seeking distractions of various kinds—taking risks, using drugs, overeating, and so on. Many of these work temporarily, but they also have unpleasant long-term consequences.

Many who are tormented by their voices would gladly volunteer for brain surgery to silence them. Although our internal voices are learned from other people in the real world, when we recall them they are inside us, so they are a part of us, a part of our own neurology. If we were successful in removing them, we would also remove all the positive things they can do for us, and we would become less whole, less capable, and less human. Eliminating a voice—even if it were possible, and even if it might make us feel better—is not a good solution.

Another quite popular and highly regarded approach is not quite as radical as silencing a voice. Many schools of psychotherapy, particularly cognitive-behavioral therapy, advocate arguing with an internal voice in order to overcome it or subdue it. If you have ever tried to argue with someone else in the real world, you have probably realized how ineffective that usually is. Typically the other person will respond by redoubling their effort to convince you, and the same is true of arguing with your internal voices. Arguing with an internal voice usually makes the voice even stronger, which is probably not what you wanted. Even if you manage to shout down a troublesome voice temporarily, you can never really overcome it, and it will return to torment you.

What *Does* Work for Transforming Negative Self-Talk

This book doesn't offer strategies for silencing a voice or arguing with it. It takes a very different approach: making small changes in how we listen to a troublesome voice.

An example of this is a wonderful video in which Michael Yapko, a therapist who specializes in depression, helps a man turn around his lifelong depression in a single hour-long session. The man's depression was caused by his memories of a childhood that was horribly abusive, both physically and verbally, and as a result he had abusive and depressing internal voices that kept him unhappy 24/7. In one segment of Michael's session with this man, he offers him several examples of how he could experience critical voices in a different and more useful way:

> When I have hundreds of people in a room, and I ask, "Who among you has good self-esteem?" hands go up—not many, but some hands go up. And then I ask them, "Do you have an inner critic? Do you have a voice inside your head that criticizes you and says rotten things to you, and puts you down, and says mean and horrible things to you?" And every single one says, "Yes."
>
> And I say to them, "If you have a voice that says rotten things to you, how can you have good self-esteem?"

> And the interesting reply—it's always a bit different—but the common bottom line is they don't listen to it. And when I ask them, "*How* do you not listen to it?" that's when I learn all sorts of different strategies.
>
> One person said, "Well, I picture it as on a volume control knob, and I just turn the volume down.
>
> Somebody else said, "I picture it as a barking dog, tied to a tree, and I just keep walking."
>
> Somebody else says, "You know, I have another voice on my shoulder that says good things to me."
>
> But the interesting thing is that every single person has that inner critic, that critical voice. It's just a question of whether they listen to it or not. (Yapko, 2001, pp. 129–130)

These are just a few of the many ways that ordinary people have learned—usually unconsciously and by chance—how to listen to a critical voice in a way that is useful to them. Although Yapko says, "It's just a question of whether they listen to it or not," I think this is not quite accurate. What is really going on is that they found a different way to listen to it, one that diminished the intensity of the voice, rather than trying to eliminate it altogether.

Refocusing Attention

When you have an unpleasant internal voice and you feel bad in response, it is natural to want to escape it, so that you can feel better. One very ancient way to do this is to learn how to attend to something else, allowing the voice to recede into the background of your awareness. At any moment we attend to only a very few aspects of our experience. For instance, as you have been reading this book, you probably have not been paying attention to the sounds around you, some of which may have been quite loud or repetitive.

Pause now for a moment to listen to the sounds that you have been ignoring. . . .

You didn't have to deliberately ignore these sounds—and if you did try to do that, it probably resulted in paying even more attention to them. When you were focused on reading this book, the sounds around you simply faded into the background of your awareness. They were still there, but when you were not attending to them, you didn't notice them, and they didn't affect you.

Now focus your attention on your bodily feelings—your posture, the temperature of your skin, your breathing, and so on. . . .

As you do this, you may find that parts of your body have been in one position too long and have become a bit stiff or tense, motivating you to shift your position a bit to relieve that. Even when you are attending to your bodily feelings, you have probably been ignoring some of the messages coming in from different parts of your body, like the small of your back, the soles of your feet, the backs of your knees, and so on. However, as soon as I mention those parts, you have to notice them in order to understand my words. You have only so much attention; as you attend to those bodily sensations, it withdraws attention from other feelings, and from the sounds around you, and all the other things that you could be aware of.

If you are watching an engrossing movie or reading a fascinating book, you may find yourself almost completely oblivious to your bodily sensations and events around you. This principle, called *figure-ground* or *foreground-background*, has even been used by hypnotists for over a hundred years to help people deal with intense chronic pain, teaching them how to attend to other aspects of their ongoing experience, so that the pain can recede into the background of awareness.

Refocusing your attention in this way is one way to diminish how much you attend to an internal troublesome voice. However, it is usually temporary, and when the voice comes back, its message is usually just as unpleasant.

Focusing on the Present Moment

Most of our problems and difficulties don't exist in the here and now; they are usually either memories of the past, or thoughts about what might be happening right now in some other place, or thoughts about the future. In many ancient meditative traditions, attention is focused on some aspect of our present experience—the breathing, or a candle flame, or a religious icon—to withdraw attention from whatever is troubling you.

Our memories of past troubles only exist insofar as we resurrect them and bring them into the present moment. It is too bad that they happened even once; continuing to recall them means that they keep happening over and over again. Wasn't once already too much? Elizabeth Smart was kidnapped, tied to a tree, and sexually abused for 9 months in 2002 when she was 14. After being rescued, she said that the key to her readjustment was letting go of the hate she felt toward her abductors. She said, "Nine months of my life was taken from me, and I wasn't going to give them any more of my time." That is a very useful attitude for anyone who has had bad experiences, freeing her from having to reexperience them over and over again. However, the instruction to let go of an experience is something that many people find difficult or impossible to do.

This morning I was troubled by a potential legal problem that could result in the loss of a considerable amount of money. Although that was a problem in the real world, and I needed to do something about it, it did not actually exist in the present moment.

I had not yet lost any money; that was only a possibility that might occur in the future. As Mark Twain observed, "I've suffered a great many catastrophes in my life. Most of them never happened." Once I had done what I could to prevent the possible future problem, it made sense to return to the present moment, where everything was fine and I could relax.

Another way to refocus attention on the present moment is to engage in a sport or some other activity that requires us to be in the present. If you are hitting or catching a fast-moving ball, you have to perceive it in the moment in order to do that. If you are cutting down a tree with a chain saw, you really need to attend to the saw, and which way the tree is likely to fall. Once I knew a woman whose guru told her to get a job chopping vegetables in a Chinese restaurant, a job that required her to chop vegetables very fast, with a very large and very sharp knife. That motivated her internal critical voices to be silent so that she could attend to the present moment and avoid losing some fingers.

Attending to anything in the present tends to withdraw our attention from an internal voice that talks about the past or future, or about present events in some other place. Learning how to redirect our attention in this way can free us from being helpless prisoners of our thoughts. This undoubtedly accounts for the popularity—and immense variety—of mindfulness and other programs that advocate learning how to "be in the here and now," some of which are thousands of years old.

The major difficulty with most meditative methods is that they typically take years of practice, and many people find them only partly effective. Another difficulty is that the idea of being in the present moment has sometimes become a universal prescription, applied to all self-talk, whether negative or positive. A voice that remembers a horrible past can also remind you of treasured memories and satisfying successes; a voice that predicts future failure and misery can also encourage you by forecasting pleasure and happiness. If you were always in the present moment, you would lose an extremely valuable source of support and optimism that can help carry you through rough times.

Internal voices can be very destructive and disorganizing, or they can be very useful and supportive—and everything in between. This book will help you become aware of how you talk to yourself, and how you can change that in order to feel differently. We will be exploring a number of ways that you can quickly and easily transform your negative self-talk into something positive and useful, sometimes literally in seconds.

By reading these pages and doing the simple exercises offered here, you can learn many different ways to easily and quickly change your own inner voices to enhance your life and make each day a more positive experience.

1. First you will learn how to identify the inner voices that have been causing you trouble, and how to listen to them carefully.
2. Then you will learn a variety of ways to rapidly change both the words, and how you say those words, to make your life work better.
3. You will also learn to recognize what kinds of changes will actually improve your life, and what kinds of changes might appear to be useful but would actually cause you more trouble in the long run.

In this book I have collected and presented a wide variety of ways to transform negative internal self-talk, learned from over 35 years of training and research. Much of this has come from others who have taught me, or contributed ideas, while some of it has come in little "Ah ha!" moments in assisting someone, or reviewing a communication or a transcript of a session. Others I have learned from participants in training seminars. All these little bits and pieces had to be set down and then fit together into a coherent whole. In order to do this, I had to have a supportive and creative inner voice that would continually suggest what words, phrases, and sentences to use in writing, and offer better alternatives when editing.

Most people pay attention to the words that an internal voice says, and it can often be very useful to change those words. However, the nonverbal sounds that are used to convey those words are often much more important than the words themselves, and they are often much easier and simpler to change. For simplicity and ease of understanding, each chapter is devoted to one or two methods for doing this, beginning with changing some nonverbal aspects of a voice, which can be surprisingly rapid and effective. So we will start there, with how a voice speaks, and only later show how to change what a voice says.

1 Changing Location

Almost everyone can easily think of a troublesome voice, but very few people take the time to really listen to it and notice where it is located in their personal space. The location of a voice turns out to be a major aspect of its impact on you, and it is one of the easiest things to change.

Listen now to a troublesome voice that makes you feel bad in some way, and notice its location in your personal space. Most voices are located either somewhere inside your head or in the space immediately surrounding your head. . . .

Is it located somewhere inside your head or outside? . . .

Is it in front or behind, left side or right side, above or below? . . .

And which way it is pointed—toward you, away from you, or somewhere in between? . . .

Take a little more time to identify all these different aspects of the location of your voice. It may help to first gesture with a hand or finger to indicate where the voice is, and the direction it is pointed, and then find a way to describe what you discovered. . . .

Changing Direction

When a troublesome voices is located outside your head, it is almost always pointed toward your head. Now that you know the location and direction of your troublesome voice, you can experiment with some changes and notice how these changes alter your response to it. First change the way the voice is pointing and find out how this changes your experience of the voice. For most people this is quite easy; it is just not something they ever thought of doing. If you have any difficulty, simply allow that voice to change direction. First try allowing that voice to reverse direction (usually this will make it point directly away from the head) and find out what that is like. . . .

Then find out what it is like to listen to the voice when it is pointing halfway between pointing toward you and away from you. . . .

Notice if there is any difference between when it is pointing straight up and straight down. . . .

Or between pointing left and right. . . .

Or forward and back. . . .

When the voice is pointing away from you, usually the volume is less, and your response to it is less intense. Most people feel better when a troubling voice is pointing away from them, and this makes it easier and more comfortable to listen to what the voice is saying. When it is pointing halfway between those extremes, the intensity of your response is usually somewhere in between when it is pointing toward you and away from you.

Note

Notice that I used the words *usually* and *most people* in the previous paragraph. I often offer generalizations about how people respond to their internal voices, based on my experience of making these kinds of changes with a large number of people. However, you may sometimes have a different response than what I present here.

Whenever your response is different than what I describe, that is very important information. Your response is yours, no matter what I may say is "usually true" for "most people." If you experience something different, that isn't wrong; it's just that your mind works somewhat differently than that of "most people." As long as you discover how your mind works, you can use this information to have more choices. I will be offering you many changes to try out, so that you can find out what works for you—even if it is different from what most other people experience. Whenever you discover a change that is useful, that adds to your choices about how a voice sounds and how you feel in response to it.

Simply changing the direction of the voice is only one small way that you can learn how to have some control over the intensity of your response to it, and this is a choice that you can now make at any time. Now return your voice to its original direction, so that you can discover other ways that you can change your response to a voice. . . .

Changing Location Inside Your Body

First, listen to the voice again, and notice your feeling response. . . .

Is it any different than when you began reading this chapter? . . .

Now experiment with changing the location of the voice in a variety of ways, to experience the impact of hearing the same voice coming from different locations in space, and how your feelings change when you do this. Again, most people find this quite easy; it is just not something they ever thought of doing. If you have any difficulty, simply allow that voice to change its location.

Hear that voice as if it were coming from your left elbow, and notice what that is like. . . .

Most people find that when their critical voice comes from their elbow, it is less impactful. The voice may also spontaneously change in tonality when you do this, perhaps becoming quieter and higher pitched, and your feelings probably also become less intense.

Next I want to offer you a number of other choices about where you hear that voice coming from. Some of them will probably make the voice less unpleasant, while others may make it more unpleasant. Your job is to simply to try out each suggestion that I offer you, and pause to discover how it changes your experience.

Now hear this voice coming from your stomach or belly, and notice how you respond to it. . . .

Now hear the voice coming from your right kneecap, and notice how you respond to it. . . .

Next, hear that voice speaking from your heart, and notice how you respond to it. . . .

Now hear that voice coming from your left big toe, and notice how you respond to it. . . .

Next, experiment with hearing that voice coming from some other part of your body, and find out how you respond to it. . . .

Finally, return that voice to its original location and direction. . . .

Pause to notice if your response to what the voice says in its original location is the same now as before you tried these experiments, or whether it is somewhat different now. . . .

Typically, hearing an unpleasant voice in locations more distant from your head will be more comfortable to listen to, and locations near or inside your head will be most unpleasant. Hearing a troublesome voice coming from the stomach is usually unpleasant, and the feeling that results may be confused with hunger, loneliness, or nausea. Hearing a troublesome voice coming from your heart may be particularly unpleasant and confusing. Some people actually do this without realizing it, and it is not particularly useful in helping them live productive lives. I have asked you to experiment with hearing a troublesome voice coming from your stomach or heart only to give you an experience of the importance of location, not because I think it is a good thing to do.

Next review the results of these little experiments and ask yourself, "In which location was it most comfortable for me to listen to this troubling voice?" . . .

Now hear the voice coming from that location, and then combine this with what you discovered previously about the direction of the voice. Change the direction of the voice so that it improves your feeling response the most. . . .

Changing Location Outside Your Body

Now hear that voice coming from outside your body. First hear it from 2 feet in front of your face. . . .

And then 10 feet in front of you. . . .

And then 30 feet in front of you. . . .

And then 100 feet in front of you. . . .

And then even farther away than that. . .

Usually a voice that is farther away will be less impactful and easier to listen to. Distance often also changes the volume of the voice and may also change its tonality. Although distance alone is usually a useful way to reduce the impact of a voice, changing direction can also be important, and you can also experiment with that.

Now hear the voice behind you, and again experiment with hearing it 2, 10, 30, and 100 feet away and even farther. . . .

Now compare hearing the voice at the same distance in front of you and behind you, and notice any differences. . . .

Usually a voice that is behind you will be less impactful, because many people think of their past experiences as being behind them and their future experiences as being in front of them.

Next hear the voice coming from your left side, and experiment with distance in the same way—2, 10, 30, and 100 feet away and farther. . . .

Next hear the voice on your right side, and experiment with distance in the same way. . . .

Now compare hearing the voice at the same distance to your left and to your right, and notice any differences. . . .

Often a voice will be less impactful on the left than the right, because many people think of their past as being on their left, and their future as being on their right—though a significant number of people reverse this. (Often these people are left-handed or ambidextrous, and have a different—though just as good—brain organization.)

Next hear the voice above you, and experiment with distance in the same way as before. . . .

Next hear the voice below you, and do the same. . . .

Now compare hearing the voice at the same distance above you and below you, and notice any differences. . . .

I have asked you to experiment with hearing the voice in the six main spatial dimensions, but of course there are an infinite number of other possible directions. If you experiment with some other direction in relation to your body, you may find a way to change the impact of the voice even more. . . .

In the foregoing, I have assumed that you hear the voice coming from a single location in space. However, it would be possible to hear it coming from two or more places in space simultaneously, and some people do this spontaneously. If you are feeling adventurous, you could try that. . . .

When a voice comes from two or more locations, it is likely to make your feelings in response to it even more intense, as if two or more people were yelling at you at the same time. On the other hand, hearing a voice coming simultaneously from different locations might make it seem unreal and comical, which would decrease its intensity.

Yet another possibility is that the voice could be coming from all directions at once, as if the entire universe was shouting at you. As in the previous experiment, this could increase the intensity of your response exponentially, or you might find it humorous to think that the entire universe was shouting at you.

Why does location matter so much, and why does moving a voice farther away from your head usually make it less disturbing and easier to listen to? When something threatens us in the real world, if it is closer to us, we need to respond more quickly and intensely to protect ourselves. If a threat is farther away, we have more time to prepare a response, so it isn't quite as urgent. The same is usually also true of your internal world, which is a kind of replica, more or less, of the external world.

Difficulty in Changing Location

If you ask someone to change the location and direction of a voice, as described previously, most people can do it easily; they just never noticed the location or thought about the possibility of changing it. However, some people may find it difficult, especially if they are not familiar with paying attention to internal events and making these kinds of changes. The voice may not move, as if it were stuck in a particular location, or it may move, but immediately move back to its previous location, as if it had a mind of its own. When this occurs, it will often be helpful to change your wording. Instead of saying, "move the voice," try saying, "just watch as it moves," or "notice what happens as you allow the voice to move" and see if that kind of language makes it easier for the voice to move to a new location.

If the voice still doesn't move, or continues to immediately return to its original location when you move it, there may be a good reason, and it is best to respect this, even when you don't yet know what the reason is. If you want to explore this further, you can imagine that the voice is another person and ask it, "What is your objection to moving?" or "What would I lose if you moved into that location?" and then listen to what the voice answers.

For instance, the voice might say something like, "If you don't listen to me, you might get into trouble." If you reply to the voice, "In a different location it would be easier for me to hear what you say, and I would be more willing to listen to you," the voice may then be willing to change location, because its intention is no longer threatened.

This is only one example, but whatever the voice says to you can be the beginning of a negotiation between you and the voice that can result in more choices for you.

The Difference Between "I Am" and "You Are"

There are other ways to create separation between you and a voice that are less direct, and that anyone can do, which is easy to confirm in your own experience. Think of a self-critical voice and notice whether it says, "I am—" or "You are—" and how you feel in response. . . .

Now keep all the other words the same, but switch to the other possibility (from "I am—" to "You are—" or the reverse) and again notice any difference in how you feel in response. . . .

When a voice says, "I am [stupid, boring, etc.]" there is usually very little separation between you and the voice; the conflict is apparently within yourself, inside your own head. But when the voice says "You are [stupid, boring, etc.]" it is clear that the conflict is between you and someone else, and the voice is usually located outside your head, where it is more distant and at least a little less troubling.

When the voice is in my head, I feel a little unsettled or wiggly, as if I don't quite know who I am. Am I the voice, or am I my feelings in response to the voice? Since they are in conflict, it is hard to identify with either one. When I change from "I am—" to "You are—" the location of the voice shifts from the center of my head to a location outside my head and about a foot to the left of my left ear. This is true even when I don't have an image of anyone saying those words. When the voice is out to the side, the separation between the two sides of the conflict—between the voice and my feelings in response—is much clearer. The voice is someone else, and my feelings are mine, and even when the feelings are unpleasant I feel more solid about who I am.

Whose Voice Is This?

Now if you ask yourself, "Who is speaking to me in this way?" or "Who does that voice belong to?" that makes an even clearer separation between you and the voice that is speaking to you. This separation is not just a matter of making an intellectual distinction between self and other; it actually increases your experience of separation in space. This greater separation will usually lessen the intensity of your feeling, because a danger or challenge that is farther away from you is less immediately threatening. You can easily confirm this in your own experience. Think of a troublesome voice, and first notice what it says. . . .

Then notice whether it says, "I am—" or "You are—" . . .

If it says, "I am—" change it to "You are—" as in the previous exercise. . . .

Next notice who is speaking to you in this way, and notice if you have an image of this person who is speaking to you. (If you can't immediately identify whose voice it is, ask yourself, "If I did know, who would it be?" or "Who does this voice remind me of?) . . .

Adding an Image of the Speaker

Many people will spontaneously get an image of the speaker as a way to identify who it is. If you already have an image, notice what it is like to hear the same voice with or without this image. . . .

Usually a voice with an image will be farther away in physical location than a voice without an image. Even when this is not the case, your sense of separation is likely to be stronger, and your sense of who you are as a separate person will feel more solid.

That image of the speaker will usually be seen outside yourself, rather than inside your head. If that doesn't happen spontaneously, say to yourself, "Can I remember when this person spoke to me in this way?" You will usually see the other person outside yourself as you retrieve a memory of a specific event, in a specific context.

Adjusting the Location of the Image

This image of the person who is speaking to you may be directly in front of you, or it may be somewhat off to the side, or less often even behind you. But wherever the person is located, it will usually be facing toward you. It can be interesting to change this and notice how that changes your response. For instance, in the scene that you see, you could move behind the person who is speaking to you, so that he or she is facing away from you, or you could change the direction the person is facing, without changing anything else, and notice if this changes your response. . . .

Often your image of this other person will also be somewhat higher than you are, in a position of some kind of power or authority (or sometimes the reverse). If you notice that the other person in your image is higher, raise yourself so that you are at eye level, and notice any change in your response. . . .

If the other person is lower than you are, you can lower yourself to be at eye level, and notice any change in your response. . . .

Most people find that if the other person is higher than they are, they feel weaker and less powerful; if the other person is lower, they feel stronger and more powerful. Either imbalance will distort communication and create trouble. "Seeing eye to eye" is usually a much better way to have clear communication, and this is often evident in a change in the volume or tonality of that person's voice—it may become more reasonable or matter-of-fact and less critical or abusive. Sometimes this may also result in the voice using different words, as well.

When that person is facing you, there may be an implicit message of conflict or confrontation, rather than cooperation. Changing the person's location, the direction that he is facing, and his height in relation to you can be used to indirectly change the conflict or confrontation into something more useful, joining with it rather than confronting it, and it can be interesting to experiment with this kind of change.

For instance, try changing the person's location from wherever you saw her to being beside you at the same level, facing in the same direction, as if you were sitting together discussing something that is in front of both of you. Does that change how she is speaking to you in any way? . . .

Notice if this change to sitting together facing in the same direction makes any change in the words that that person says, and if there is any change in your feeling response to what she says. . . .

In this position, usually the other person will become more cooperative and less argumentative or confrontational. His voice may become softer or slower, and you may notice corresponding changes in your own response. Your unpleasant feelings will likely become less intense, and they may also change in quality—you may be interested rather than annoyed, confused rather than angry, or curious rather than fearful. . . .

For example, several years ago I was having lunch with a colleague at a national psychotherapy conference. She was talking about her 10-year-old son, who was having some difficulties, and about her anxiety and uncertainty about him. When I asked her where she saw the image of her son, she looked and gestured straight ahead of her, and said, "About 15 feet away." I asked her to bring this image of her son next to her, so that he was by her side, facing in the same direction. When she did this, her anxiety changed instantly to soft tears of sadness about what he was going through, and then she said calmly and confidently, "I know what to do. All I have to do is be with him and support him."

When you realize the impact of this kind of change in location, you can use it to change your response—or a client's response—to a voice. Below is a particularly graceful way to do this, described by Andrew T. Austin, a hypnotherapist in the UK, in his wonderful book, *The Rainbow Machine*:

> One technique I use a lot that has produced some results that are sometimes as dramatic as the Core Transformation process [Andreas & Andreas, 1994] came from something a psychotherapist told me that sounds much like something Virginia Satir [Andreas, 1991] might have done—maybe I read it in one of her books. In doing family therapy, she had a family where the conflict was between the father and his 17-year-old son. The father was a "strong" and stoical man, for whom expressing emotion was not an easy or desirable skill.
>
> She told the son to get up and stand behind the seated father and gently place a hand on each of his father's shoulders in order to "feel and relieve some of the tension there." Apparently this made a huge change in the relationship between father and son, so naturally it got me thinking about how this could be used for an individual, when the father or someone else is not present.
>
> As I have mentioned previously, the internal representations of problem people are rarely, if ever, radiating beauty and light. I'll often ask what the expression on their face is, and what

their posture is. Then I'll ask the client to imagine walking behind that person and gently placing a hand on each shoulder and giving just a little gentle massage to loosen them up a bit.

As the client imagines touching them, this also shifts their kinesthetic feelings. Usually the representation itself changes, relaxes, or even starts crying. For instance:

Client: "I feel criticized."

Therapist: "What has to happen inside for you to feel criticized?" (Since criticism is a largely verbal activity. I could have asked, "And who criticizes you, and what do they say?")

C: "I hear a voice."

T: "And if that voice were a person, who would that be?"

C: "My father. My father was always criticizing me; he had a horrible voice like that." (The client has not seen father for over 14 years.)

T: "And if your father were in the room now, where would he be?"

C: "Standing right in front of me, really close, facing me."

T: "That's right. Now close your eyes. I want you to imagine walking around behind him, and gently place one hand on each of his shoulders and gently massage those shoulders. Whisper into one ear that is close enough to hear you, to 'Relax now . . . all the way.' . . . Tell him it's OK, . . . it's OK, . . . Give him a few moments to relax, all the way down now. . . ."

Try this now yourself; think of someone you felt inferior to as a child, and hold that representation in mind. Then stand up, go around behind them, and gently massage their shoulders and notice the difference. . . .

This is a nice maneuver that achieves several things simultaneously. Primarily it completely shifts the spatial orientation of the client in relation to the representation. Instead of facing each other in opposition, they become oriented in the same direction, with implications of alliance and cooperation. In addition, massaging someone's shoulders and talking to them in this way presupposes a much more friendly relationship than criticism does, opening the door to a more understanding attitude.

One aspect of this is worth pointing out, as it isn't always obvious at first. When you elicit a representation from a sitting client and then ask them to stand up, the representation tends to stay where it is in geographical space. A representation that is a negative artifact from childhood is often bigger, or higher up than the client, and because of this it often represents something more powerful than the client. However, when you stand up and massage someone's shoulders, you are the same height, with implications of equality. And when you feel equal to someone else, you feel much less defensive and threatened. If that other person was originally sitting down, you may even find that you are higher than they are, with a corresponding feeling of power, instead of vulnerability.

In my early days, I would try to get the client to reduce the size of the representation, or "push" it further away. Invariably they would find some kind of difficulty. Then I chanced upon

> the move described above, which is much more graceful and effective.
>
> Essentially, this puts the client in control of the representation, and gets the representation to relax. The representation is exactly that—a representation of a part of himself, a bit of his own psyche that isn't feeling nice. This is a hugely powerful technique. I prefer to have the client remain sitting and do this in their imagination. However, it isn't unusual for someone to actually stand up and go through the physical motions of these activities. This is particularly likely if the client is an athlete, or someone else who attends closely to their body and its position in great detail. (Austin, 2007, pp. 80–81)

These examples may suggest other changes in position that could be useful with a troubling voice. What if you were both lying down side by side on chaise longues on a beach, enjoying the summer sun? Or sitting back to back? Or in some other position that would make communication easier and more productive? What change in position would be most useful for you, with the voice that you have? Pause now to try one of these alternatives, and find out how it changes your relationship to a troubling voice. . . .

These kinds of changes in position can be used in many other ways and in other contexts. Think of three or four family members, or people you interact with at work, or other people you know, and then close your eyes and visualize them around you in your personal space at the same time. Finally notice their locations and which way they are facing, their relative height in relationship to you, and so on. Pause now to do this. . . .

Probably the people with whom you have the best relationships are closer to you, more aligned with you, and at the same height, so that you are eye to eye, while the people that you have more difficulty with are farther away, perhaps facing away from you, or at a different height, and so forth. You can use this kind of visualization to become clearer about the kind of relationship you have with each of them. And if you want to, you can change the location of the people in your mind, which will tend to change how you respond to them in your mind, which in turn will often change how you interact with them in real life.

For instance, let's say you feel distant from someone, and you would like to feel closer. In your mind, you can bring the person closer, perhaps adjust which way she is facing, and so on, until you feel closer to her. When you next interact with her, you will probably respond in ways that express the kind of closeness that you want.

Or perhaps there is someone who tends to overwhelm you and tower over you in a way that leaves you little choice. You can move him further away in your mind, and lower him, so that there is more space for your own views and feelings. Then when you next meet him, you will be more self-assertive and feel more in control of events. For much more detail about exactly how to do this kind of rearrangement, see Lukas Derks's (2005) excellent book, *Social Panoramas*.

Changing Volume

Now that we have explored location thoroughly, it is time to turn to the volume of a voice, which is usually a powerful element of how it affects you. In the external world, someone who is shouting loudly is more likely to trouble you, and the same is true of your internal world. When you change the location of a negative voice so that it is farther away, you often find that the volume decreases, making it much less unpleasant to listen to the voice. Changing the volume is a major factor in making the voice easier to listen to, and changing the location in space is a way to change the volume. But how does this work so easily?

You have had many experiences in the real world in which a sound source moved away from you (or you moved away from a sound), and as it did, the sound became quieter. You have also had many experiences in which a sound moved closer to you (or you moved closer to a sound) and it got louder.

When you imagine a sound moving away, or that you are moving away from a sound, it elicits coordinated simultaneous memories in all your senses of that happening. The memories of the sound moving away correspond to a decrease in volume. In other words, remembering this kind of event elicits the same internal neurology that occurred when that happened in the external world. That same neurology can be used to make a corresponding change in your internal world.

Contrast can be a way of drawing attention to what we experience so automatically that we have a hard time noticing it—like the fish who will be the last to discover water. Imagine that you are talking to someone, and that you can hear his voice clearly. Then imagine him moving away from you rapidly, perhaps on a train, and as he becomes more distant, hear his voice becoming louder and louder. Pause to do this now. . . .

You probably found that quite hard to do, which is one indication of how unnatural it is. And if and when you succeeded, it probably seemed very strange, for the same reason.

The way that you normally experience the way volume changes with distance is called a *reference experience*; an experience in the external world that has the characteristics that you need to make a change in your internal world. Whenever you want to make a change, you can search for a memory of something happening in the external world that has the characteristics that you need in order to make the internal change. When you reexperience it fully, that will elicit the same response that you had in the external world.

This understanding opens up a world of possibilities, which skilled hypnotists have been using for a century or more to assist people in changing aspects of their experience that are not under conscious control. For instance, if you want to lower the temperature in your hands, or to shrink the blood vessels in them, you can vividly imagine putting them in a bucket of ice water; if you want to raise the temperature of your hands, or dilate the blood vessels in them, you can imagine putting them into a bucket of hot water.

If your goal is to decrease the volume of a voice, you can think of many other contexts in which the volume changed as a result of some event, or something that you did. Pause now to think of several events in the real world (other than increasing distance) that decreased the volume of a sound or voice. . . .

Can you think of a time when someone was talking to you and then closed a door between you? Or drew a curtain? Or the person speaking to you turned away from you, or put her head under the covers? Or you covered your ears with your hands? If you were in a bathtub, submerging your ears would muffle the sound. You can use any experience like this to change volume, as long as it is something that you have experienced, preferably repeatedly.

Earlier you experimented with changing the location, direction, and distance of a troublesome voice to make it much more comfortable to listen to. When you make these kinds of changes, what you are actually doing is taking action to change your relationship to the voice. This is something that you can do voluntarily any time you want, in order to have a more resourceful response to it, giving you some control over your experience. Since a change in location, direction, or volume is a pure process change, you can use it with any voice, or any sentence, phrase, or other set of words or sounds that a voice might say.

What you have been experimenting with are changes in aspects of a voice that are usually unconscious but can become conscious if you pay attention to them or ask the right kind of question. Once you are aware of these choices, you can experiment with making changes in them. When you find a change that you are pleased with, you can then allow that change to become unconscious and automatic again, freeing your attention for other, more interesting things. You are taking the first small, yet significant, steps toward having more choice about how you think about and respond to a troublesome voice.

Two Very Important Warnings

Respect Signals of Objections or Concerns

In the introduction, when I asked you to try hearing a negative voice coming from your stomach or your heart, you probably felt worse, as most people do. That feeling was a clear signal that some part of you objected to that change, because it wasn't a useful thing to do. Some call this intuition; others call it "listening to your wiser self," or some other such phrase. Whatever you call it, it is useful feedback information, and I want you to pay attention to it and respect it. If you tried to ignore or override it, that would be a mistake—and sometimes it would be a big mistake.

You may also find that some of the changes that you made were not permanent, and that a voice spontaneously moved back to its original location, direction, or volume. This is often a signal that the change you made was not as useful as you might have thought. You can try any experiment briefly for the purpose of learning, but when you make a change that feels worse, it is very important to respect that, and change the voice back to what it was like before the experiment, and try something else.

At other times, you may find that a voice changes spontaneously, without your intention. As you were experimenting, some unconscious aspect of you discovered a useful change that you hadn't thought of or intended. Always respect this kind of spontaneous change as a signal that some other aspects of your functioning are wiser than your conscious one.

If the Voice Disappears

As you try these experiments—and the others in the chapters that follow—you may occasionally find that a voice entirely disappears, or you may find a way to deliberately make it disappear, for instance, by moving the voice so far away into the distance that you can't hear it at all.

Sometimes when a voice disappears, that is an indication that it has reorganized in some way so that it no longer needs to talk to you. Perhaps it has become completely integrated into who you are in a useful way. When this happens, you will not only feel relief from what it has been saying, you will likely also feel an added solidity, a feeling of being more whole than you were before.

However, at other times the voice may have been overcome, or smothered, or hidden, but not integrated, and it will likely emerge later to cause trouble again. When this kind of disappearance occurs, you may feel relief, but there will be a feeling of shakiness or instability, instead of the solidity that comes with integration.

Despite its unpleasantness, a troublesome voice often has some very important information or protective function for you. If you lost the voice, you would also lose that information or protection; you would lose a part of yourself, and possibly something that was very valuable, which is what usually results in a shaky feeling.

To avoid this, I always like to bring the voice back in and find a location and direction that makes it possible to comfortably hear what it is saying. That way you can talk with it and find out if the voice might still have some important message for you. If it does, you can continue to modify the voice in some way, using some of the other methods in this book. If the voice calmly and congruently tells you that it has nothing more to say to you, then you can safely allow it to disappear again. The overall goal of this book is to teach you how to transform a troublesome voice into something much more useful and supportive, but not to eliminate it.

Using Location in a Positive Way

You have experimented with how to change a troublesome voice in order to make it less impactful. That same information can be used in reverse to make a positive voice more impactful. For instance, you may have an inner knowing that says something like, "Whatever happens, I am a worthwhile person." "I know I am capable and resourceful." Or "I know I am loved." If this voice is far away and quiet, and doesn't sound very convincing to you, try moving it closer and making it louder. You could try putting that voice into your heart, your chest, or your belly, and find out if that produces a stronger feeling of truth and conviction. Or you can try any other change that you find increases the impact of that positive voice.

However, you need to be very careful when you do this, so please be very cautious and extra sensitive to any concerns or objections. You also need to be very careful about the words that you use, and I want you to know how to avoid these problems before you do much with adding or changing the words that you say to yourself.

For instance, if you have a supportive voice that is in opposition to a troublesome one, making the supportive one stronger can escalate the conflict, which often causes problems. If a troublesome voice says, "You're stupid," and you add a voice that says, "I'm smart," those voices are in direct opposition.

However, if you add a voice that says, "I can learn how to be smart," that voice is not in opposition, because a stupid person can learn to be smart. In fact the implication of "I can learn to be smart" is that the person is not already smart, which is in agreement with the voice that says, "I'm stupid," so there is no conflict.

Small changes in wording like this can be very important to avoid creating conflict. There are some very important criteria for the words that a resourceful voice says to make sure that it really works well to support you. When you learn what those are, you can make changes that won't backfire or cause problems that could be worse than the one you wanted to solve.

Another possibility is to first transform a troublesome voice and then strengthen a supportive one. Avoiding conflict not only makes change much more comfortable, it makes it much easier to do, and the changes will be much more lasting and useful.

In later chapters we will return to using the information in this chapter positively. I discuss many other ways to change what a voice says in great detail in later chapters, particularly Chapters 4, 7, 9, and 10. But first I want to explore simple ways to change other nonverbal aspects of a voice and its emotional impact on you. The first of these is to change the tempo or tonality.

2 Changing Tempo & Tonality

Think of a simple sentence like, "I need to get going," and hear it in your mind in an ordinary, everyday tempo. . . .

Now say the exact same sentence internally in a very fast tempo. . . .

Finally, say it in a very slow tempo, even slower than if you were about to nod off to sleep. . . .

Did you notice any difference in your response to that sentence in the different tempos? . . .

Most people will feel only a little motivated by the ordinary tempo, much more motivated by the fast tempo, and completely unmotivated by the slow tempo. Since the words spoken are exactly the same, this difference is solely a result of the change in tempo. But since most people only notice the words that they speak to themselves, this effect of tempo is usually completely unconscious.

In the real world, a fast tempo is usually paired with urgent situations in which we need to tense up and do something quickly, while a slow tempo is typically associated with relaxation, rest, and leisure activities. Since we use our memories of those real-world events to construct our internal world, a fast tempo usually elicits tension and motivation, while a slow tempo elicits relaxation and repose. However, if you had a parent who motivated you with dire threats in a slow voice, you might be very motivated by a slow tonality. Changing the tempo of an internal voice is another way to change the emotional impact of what you say to yourself.

Recently I saw an older woman whose dearly loved husband had died 2 years earlier, and she had been depressed ever since. I used my grief resolution process (Andreas, 2002) with her, but it was only partly successful. A little exploration revealed that she had an internal voice that was depressing her. In a low, slow voice, it said things like, "It doesn't matter; things aren't worthwhile; they don't have any meaning anymore, because you're just going to die anyway." Try saying those words to yourself in a slow tempo, over and over again, and notice how they affect you. . . .

Now send that voice off into the distance, and shake off any depressed feelings by wiggling your body a bit and then remind yourself of something that you enjoy a lot. . . .

When I asked this woman to speed up the tempo of this voice, she immediately started chuckling and said, "It became a hip-hop rapper voice." Changing the tempo resulted in changing the tonality, and the words became humorous and somewhat ridiculous, lifting her depression.

Nick Kemp is a hypnotherapist in England who has explored the use of voice tempo changes with his clients in great detail. He has originated and developed a detailed and dependable process for using tempo with anxiety and other intense and fast-paced, uncomfortable emotions that is very widely useful. It is one of the methods that Nick includes in what he terms "Provocative Change Works" (Andreas, 2008). I reproduce it on the following pages (pp. 26–37) with his permission.

Internal Voice Tempo Change

Whenever I (Nick) see someone with a problem, I always ask myself the question, "How do they do that?" I began to realize that there are a number of elements that are very similar in a wide range of conditions, which on the surface may seem very different, but actually are not that different when taking a closer look at their internal structure. With many problems that create anxiety and tension, someone is almost always talking to themselves in a fast tempo that creates and sustains their intense feeling response.

They are usually talking to themselves at such a fast tempo that they become hyperalert and stimulated, and aren't able to access other choices—rather like driving a car on the freeway while stuck in high gear, unable to change down into lower gears. At that fast speed, they lack choice; it's not possible for them to exit and turn off onto side roads, or stop for lunch. Slowing down the tempo of their internal voice makes it possible to have choices that simply weren't available to them when they were talking to themselves rapidly.

Congruence Check: Asking for Objections

Before beginning the exercise below, I do a thorough congruence check, to be sure it is appropriate to reduce or eliminate the anxiety or other unpleasant symptoms that they feel. If someone has very good reason to be anxious, and their anxiety keeps them out of dangerous situations, it would not be appropriate to change their feelings until and unless they had some other way to protect themselves from that actual danger.

However, often there is no real danger, only a perceived or imagined danger, or their response is to some past context, so the danger is no longer present. In order to distinguish between these different possibilities, it is important to find out if there are any positive outcomes that would be affected by eliminating the anxiety.

The simplest way to do this is to ask, "Does any part of you have any objection to having a more comfortable response in all the situations in which you have had these intense feelings?" Often an objection will emerge as an uncomfortable feeling or nonverbal incongruence. At other times, it may appear as an image of a potential problem, or an internal voice that is more explicit. "If I lost my anxiety, others would expect me to take charge and be more responsible." Any objection needs to be satisfied before proceeding, or it will tend to interfere with the process.

Whenever you find an objection, one option is to simply stop what you are doing until you have more experience with adjusting a voice, or until you have more experience with satisfying an objection. This is the safest option, but it prevents you from trying some changes that could be very useful.

Another option is to proceed with the process, with the full knowledge that any change can be reversed if it turns out to be unsatisfactory. If you assure any objection—whether that is a vague feeling, or a more specific image or internal voice—that you agree to reverse any change if it objects to it later, it can be comfortable trying out a change to find out if it is satisfactory or not. This option is particularly useful when an objection is not based on a specific perceived danger, but only on a somewhat vague fear of the unknown—what might possibly happen if the change was made.

Other objections are much more specific. For instance, "If I lost my anxiety, I wouldn't get out of dangerous situations fast enough," describes a protective function that needs to be respected. The simplest way to satisfy this objection would be to agree to keep the anxious feeling in any contexts that are truly dangerous, while exploring alternatives in other contexts.

Most anxiety doesn't actually protect people by keeping them out of a context that is perceived as dangerous; it only makes them feel bad while they are in it. For instance, many people are anxious about flying, but it's not strong enough to keep them from flying. It only makes them miserable when they are on a plane. Once you have decided to risk getting on a plane, the anxiety is useless, so you may as well enjoy the trip. This is an example of contextual reframing using time as the marker.

Yet another way to satisfy an objection is to ask the objection how it could be satisfied. "OK, you want to protect me from danger; how can you continue to protect me from danger, while allowing me to feel more comfortable?" In many ways this is the best option of all, because it gives the objecting part the task of finding a solution. Since it knows most about exactly what it wants to protect you from, it is in the best position to propose an effective solution.

Slowing Tempo Exercise Outline

In the outline below, sentences in *italics* and quotes give the exact language that I use, with explanatory remarks in parentheses, or in plain text.

1. Accessing the Internal Voice *"Now I know from what you have told me that up until this point you have experienced this intense feeling on a number of occasions. I'd like you to bring one of these times to mind now, and let me know what you are either thinking or saying to yourself at these times, just before the feeling occurs. You can do this either with your eyes open or closed. Most people find it easier with their eyes closed."*

Notice that this language is more immediate and associated than, "Think of a time when—" which is more ambiguous, and could result in clients thinking of an experience by seeing themselves in it, rather than being in the experience and reexperiencing what they feel when that happens. Or they might run through a listing process, scanning across different examples, but without stepping into any of them. Either of these alternatives would make it more difficult to hear what they are saying to themselves.

Usually they are able to tell me immediately what they are saying to themselves, but sometimes they may have some difficulty. If they don't know what they are saying to themselves, they may be too separated from the experience at the moment, and this is often visible in their nonverbal behavior—their body is relatively motionless, and they don't look anxious. When this is the case, there are several choices.

One choice is to use my language to help them reassociate into the experience. *"When you are in that experience, what do you feel in your body? If you are sitting down, can you feel the shape, texture, and temperature of that particular chair, and your posture as you sit in it? If you are standing, can you feel how your feet contact the floor, and the position of your feet? Do you feel tense or relaxed, balanced or off balance?"* Usually that will enable them to really be in that experience, making it easy to notice what they are saying to themselves. However, sometimes it is easier to accept and utilize their separation from the problem experience by asking them to imagine that they could see an image of themselves in the problem context. *"If I were to draw a picture of you in one of these experiences, as in a comic book, where the artist draws thought bubbles above each character's head, what should I put in the bubble over your head to indicate what is being thought at that precise moment?"*

Or you can use some version of the "as if" frame: *"If you did know what you are saying to yourself in that situation, what might it be?"* or simply, *"That's OK, just make up something."* Since I will be adjusting the tempo, not the content, the exact content of what the voice says is really not that important. It is only important that clients come up with something that fits well for them in that situation.

Once they know what they are saying to themselves, I ask them to think of other situations in which they have that feeling, and ask what they are saying to themselves then. Typically it is either the same sentence, or one that is fundamentally similar, or has the same kind of presuppositions or implications—that they are about to die, or are in some kind of very difficult situation that they can't handle, or a situation that has very unpleasant consequences. By doing this, I am helping them to create a larger category of experiences in which they have the same feeling. Then when I help them change the feeling in one of these, the change is much more likely to generalize to all the other experiences in the category.

2. Noticing the Tempo *"So the sentence you have said to yourself is, 'The plane is going to crash into the sea.' When you have said this to yourself, do you say it in your normal conversational speaking voice, or do you say this at a faster tempo?"*

Here I am offering the client just two options; most will immediately confirm that they are using a faster tempo of speaking. If they say it's otherwise, I ask them to check; to date out of the more than 900 clients I have done this with, all but two have been able to notice a much faster tempo. Those two noticed a much slower tempo, and for them I had to reverse the instructions below, teaching them to use a faster tempo instead of a slower one.

3. Baseline Tempo *"OK, now I am going to ask you to do three things. The first is to say or think this sentence exactly as you have done to date and notice how you feel in response to doing this."* . . .

4. Slowing Tempo by One Third *"OK, now I am going to say your sentence, slowed down by about one third. After I have said it, I want you to say or think this sentence to yourself at this slowed-down speed and notice what's different."* . . .

Then I say their sentence out loud and slowed down, and then pause while they say it internally in the same tempo. In order to slow down the tempo they have to change their physiology—slow their breathing, relax the tension in their vocal cords and chest, how they pronounce their words, and so on.

5. Even Slower Tempo *"OK, now I am going to say the same sentence even slower, and when I am done I want you to do the same, and let me know when you have done so."*

I then say the sentence out loud, and slow down the tempo dramatically, to demonstrate exactly what I want them to do. I allow at least two seconds between each pair of words, matching each word to their breathing out, so that each word is paired with the relaxation that naturally occurs when breathing out.

I watch them carefully to observe their increased tension as they anticipate when they will hear the next word, so that I can say the next word somewhat later than they expect. I pause even longer between the last two words of the sentence—at least double the length of the previous pauses. Then I pause to give them time to say the sentence in this slowed-down tempo, and wait for them to tell me when they are done. . . .

6. Testing *"OK, now when you try to think of this as you used to, what are you noticing that is different?"* Usually their feeling of anxiety will be entirely gone; sometimes it will be greatly reduced. The tempo shift deconstructs the meaning of the old sentence, and changes their response. Very rarely it may not change much—or at all—and I follow with the visual variation below.

Visual Variation

Another way to do the same exercise is to ask clients to see the sentence in front of them as they say it to themselves, transforming it from the auditory to the visual.

"Now I want you to see that sentence out in front of you, as if it's on a small billboard, and notice what the sentence looks like in detail. Tell me how far away from you it is,

what size the letters are, whether they in bold face, italics, or regular type, etc.". . .

"Now I want you to begin to stretch the sentence apart, creating longer spaces in between the words, first noticing the new locations of the words, and then attending to the spaces in between the words, rather than the words themselves." . . .

This is a figure/ground shift of attention. If I don't see a dramatic shift in clients' breathing and posture, sometimes I ask them to put space between the letters as well as the words. *"Now I want you to separate the letters in each word. Put spaces between the letters, and then pay attention to the spaces between the letters, rather than to the letters."* This further changes the meaning of the sentence, and is also a demonstration that they can voluntarily change their feeling response.

If the sentence has a negation in it, like "I can't—" I have sometimes suggested: *"Remove the apostrophe and the t in the second word of the sentence,"* being very careful not to say the word that I am referring to. This reverses the meaning of the sentence entirely, and they find themselves able to do what they previously thought they couldn't. I often delete any other word that causes a problem, for instance: *"And now take the fourth word, and do the same thing. Start to fade it out a little bit more, a little bit more. And then there's a certain point where—pfff—white it out. So it's not there. You know it's not there, because when you look now, it's not there."* When doing this it is important to not say the word, but only refer to it indirectly by its position in the sentence. Sometimes I will ask clients to run both the auditory and visual versions of this exercise at the same time.

Kinesthetic Tactile Variation

An additional variant is to ask clients to reach out and feel the words and letters in front of them, as if the words are solid and they can touch them with their fingers, translating from the auditory or visual systems to the kinesthetic. Then I ask them to use their hands and fingers to spread out the words—and then sometimes to also spread out the letters—and to feel the empty space between them.

In some cases I will ask them to run the kinesthetic variation along with the auditory or visual versions of this exercise at the same time, or even all three at once.

After doing this process, it is imperative to do a thorough testing and congruence check, by carefully rehearsing and testing the new response in all the different contexts in which clients previously had the old response. *"Imagine that you encounter one of these situations next week. Notice how you experience this now, and also notice if any part of you has any objections to having this new response."* Any concerns or objections need to be respected and satisfied in order to preserve any other useful outcomes that may have been served by the old response. This could include keeping the old anxious response in certain contexts to maintain the protection there. Usually an even better solution is to elicit or teach some kind of successful coping behavior in those contexts that are still perceived as dangerous, so that clients no longer need the anxious response.

The verbatim transcript that follows is from a session that I did with a professional trombonist who got anxious whenever he played in an orchestra. In this example, I utilize aspects of two of the variations described above. The transcript begins with me talking to Fred (his name has been changed).

Session Transcript

Nick: When people come to see me, they're mostly in some kind of state of anxiety. They don't come because they think, "What shall I do? I've nothing else to do. I know—I'll just go and see Nick today."

Fred: Yeah.

Nick: So they arrive with something, number one. Number two, it's something that they're doing over and over again, so no matter how much they've thought about it, they don't feel any different.

Fred: Right.

Nick: So they've got to the point when they decide to see me, they're really thinking, "You know what, I've got to do something different."

Fred: Yep.

Nick: So everything's reached a bit of a boiling point.

Fred: Yeah.

Nick: Now most of the time, what they're experiencing is the end—the final behavior at the end of the sequence. So, the final behavior is, you know, doing *this* (gestures at waist height). And before you get to that, you have how a person *feels* (gestures at chest height). And before you get to the feeling, you have what happens *here* (gestures at head height), which is what they're thinking, and how they're thinking about it. Because you can't just get a feeling.

Fred: No.

Nick: You know, if I said to you, "I want you to feel wildly enthusiastic," but you're not allowed to picture anything, look at anything, think anything to yourself, or hear anything, you can't get from the state that you're in to that state.

Fred: No, no.

Nick: There's got to be some translation here.

Fred: Yeah.

Nick: So here's the good news: In order to change the final result, you've got to change this stuff up here.

Fred: Yeah.

Nick: So it's the way in which you think and how you think that creates the feeling, that then creates the end behavior.

Fred: Right.

Nick: So, we'll explore some of that. Now, somebody goes to somebody, and they get some kind of relief for a short period of time, then usually that means it's not been contextualized enough. So the person feels totally relaxed during the session and goes, "Yeah, yeah, yeah, all is well," and so on. And they go away and then they go, "OK, what's the first number? (Fred laughs.) Stravinsky's *Firebird*. Damn." And you start thinking to yourself, "Is it gonna go well? Is it gonna go well?" And then, "Oh, well, now I'm starting to run the anxiety program." Think this in anxious voice, probably a fast anxious voice, start to get a feeling which could be here or here (gesturing toward his chest and belly area), then start to think, now you're feeling anxious, then you start to think, usually predictive things, "What if?" or future tense, or future case things. All anxiety is about anticipation. Now, I'm not even in the orchestra; I'm already feeling anxious.

Fred: That's right. Yeah.

Nick: I'm running through my head scenarios of different things. Now I'm thinking, "Maybe I could just run." (Fred laughs loudly.) So, the states that people crank up, in terms of their feeling states, are through the process. The secret is to unravel the process, so people can get what's appropriate for them. Because it's all very nice and delightful for someone to say, "Hey, a bit of adrenalin is no bad thing." And you go, "Step into *my* head for a day.

Fred: Yeah.

Nick: And see how that feels, and then tell me if that's the same thing."

Fred: Yeah.

Nick: Because if you're sitting there thinking, "Uhhhhh," over and over again in the same way, then as somebody who is a performer and who's measured on their final ability to perform, I know that this is like, "I can get through it." But I don't want to be sort of like, you know, sort of "just getting through it," I want to be enjoying what I'm doing.

Fred: Yeah, absolutely.

Nick: Because, chances are, if you're doing it in rehearsals, exactly the same music, exactly the same plays, even if you're sitting in the same seat inthe same theater, with the same conductor and the same musicians, it would be absolutely fine—because you're not running the same process.

Fred: Yeah, yeah.

Nick: Sound familiar?

Fred: Absolutely correct, on all counts (laughs).

Nick: Somebody said to me, "How did you know that?" I said, "Well, just luck." Well, also, once you've seen your first thousand clients, then you realize there's really only going to be a few things. Well, let's just—I have an instinct over how you're doing this. And, as I said to one client, "I wouldn't want to bet against me, because I'm usually right." (Fred laughs.) So, the sort of things that you think to yourself are: "Is it going to go well?" That's one that you mentioned. What other things are going through your head?

Fred (taking a deep breath): I unconsciously sort of think about sitting there and the worst things happening—notes not being produced—

Nick (overlapping): Like what? Forgot to get dressed?

Fred: Well, no, not that (laughter).

Nick: The job is a trombone, not a triangle; that could be really problematic.

Fred: Just, just, you know, not being to produce notes or splitting notes, not producing very well, or just the anticipation of sitting there almost frozen with nerves, really.

Nick: OK, these are all descriptions of what could happen. What I'm interested in is—just close your eyes for a second. Now, pick one of the times when you had the anxiety in the past. Now what I'm interested in is, what—first person—is going through your head? So if I was going to draw a cartoon of you, and write some bubbles above your head, what do I actually put in the bubbles that Fred is thinking to himself?

Fred: "Oh shit, I don't wanna be here."

Nick: "Oh shit, I don't wanna be here." All right. Now, is that a familiar phrase?

Fred: Umm, yes, I think it is, really.

Nick: OK. And keep your eyes closed, and just check. Is it said in an anxious kind of thought, in an anxious kind of a voice, and a quick kind of a voice? Just say, "Yes."

Fred: Yes, it is.

Nick: Saves time really, it's like a rhetorical question. OK, so keep your eyes closed. Because the first thing we're going to do is to start sorting some of this out. So think it as you have thought it: "Oh shit, I don't wanna be here," in that same quick, anxious kind of voice that you have up until now used. . . . And when you think it to yourself like that, what do you notice?

Fred: Tension.

Nick: OK. And where do you notice the tension?

Fred: In my arms, and—

Nick: Where else?

Fred: Chest. Arms. Pretty much all over.

Nick: Where does it start, the tension?

Fred: In the chest area.

Nick: And where does it go to? . . . Does it go to the head?

Fred: Well, down the arms and up to my lips.

Nick: All right, we've got two things to work on here. Let's start with the first one. So when you think at the moment, "Oh shit, I don't want to be here" in that way, you notice it triggers the feeling.

Fred: Yeah.

Nick: Yeah? OK. So, take a deep breath in, and feel your feet flat on the floor. The next thing I want you to do is, I want you, Fred, to imagine that we're reading out of a play. So instead of how you used to think it, I want you to think it like this: You're just reading out of a script which is (flat voice), "Oh shit. I don't wanna be here." And just do that one time. Let me know you've done it. . . .

Fred: Umhmn.

Nick: OK. Now I want you to think it like a question. So think it like this: "Oh shit. I don't wanna be *here*?" (rising inflection). Run it through one time, . . . and let me know when you've done it.

Fred: Umhmn.

Nick: Now I'm going to slow down the phrase. So I'm going to put big, big gaps in between each and every word. So it'll seem like there's a pause, because there is a pause, in between each and every word. And then I want you to think it at that same slowed-down speed. And I'll say it first and I want you to think the whole phrase. Just take your time, and do it like this (each space is 2–3 seconds): "Oh . . . shit! . . . I . . . don't . . . wanna . . . be . . . here." Now slow it down to that speed (long pause). . . .

Fred: Umhmn.

Nick: OK. Now, I want you to see the phrase as if it was on a billboard in front of you. So you can see the phrase, "Oh . . . shit! . . . I . . . don't . . . wanna . . . be . . . here." And get it so that you can see each word, and you can see each word clearly. And let me know when you can see it clearly at the moment. . . .

Fred: Yeah.

Nick: Now begin to create a little bit more space between the "Oh" and the "shit," and then each and every other word. So every word is a little bit more spaced out than every other word. Just quickly run through them, so they all start to space out a little bit more. So, the first two words, and then the second two, and then the "I" and the "don't," and the "wanna," and the "be" and the "here."

Fred: Yeah.

Nick: OK. Now, take the first two words, and begin to just start to fade them out. You know when things fade out, they just get fainter and fainter and fainter . . . and then suddenly—pffft—you white them out so they're not there. And you'll know when they're not there, because when you look, they're not there. And now take the fourth word, and do the same thing. Start to fade it out a little bit more, a little bit more. And then there's a certain point where—pffft—white it out. So it's not there. You know it's not there, because when you look now, it's not there.

Fred: Umhm.

Nick: And take a deep breath in, and relax back into the space that's now there, instead. And as you feel your feet flat on the floor, you can notice now, and every time you listen back to this, just what it is that you notice that's different. Now, as you try and think about the original phrase like you used to think about it, what do you notice?

Fred: There's only four more words on the billboard.

Nick: OK. And when you think about the phrase, what effect does it have?

Fred: It's quite relaxing.

Nick: "It's quite relaxing." Now if you try and think about it like you used to think about it, what do you notice?

Fred: It doesn't have much—it doesn't have any significance.

Nick: "It doesn't have any significance." Now if you think about the time in the past when you used to think about this, in this new way, what do you notice?

Fred: It's just a memory really. Feels good, really.

Nick: "It's just a memory." OK. Now, what other phrases or things have you thought to yourself that have not been very helpful?

Fred: "Please let me play well tonight."

Nick: "Please let me play well tonight." OK. What other ones? . . . Do you say, "Is it gonna go well?" could be one of them?

Fred: Yeah.

Nick: OK. So let's just do the same thing with "Is it gonna go well?" Notice, to start with, it's a question. So, it's a questioning about whether it's gonna go well or not. Now let me just check: Is it an anxious voice, and is it a quick voice? Just say, "Yes."

Fred: Yes.

Nick: OK. Now do the same thing. Slow it down so that it's like it's out of a play. "Is it gonna go well?" Then, make it overtly a question. "Is it gonna go *well*?" (rising inflection). Then slow down the phrase so there's a big gap in between each and every word. So . . . everything . . . just . . . slows . . . down. Run it all the way through. Let me know when you've done it. . . .

Fred: Yeah.

Nick: OK. Now see it as a piece of text, but this time just fade out the first three words. Just start to fade them out more and more and more and more, and then at a certain point—pffft—white them out. So they're not there in the same way. And you'll know they're not there, because when you look they're not there.

Fred: Yeah.

Nick: Now, if you take a deep breath in and sit back in your chair, when you try to think about that phrase, what do you notice?

Fred: I just see "Go well."

Nick: "Go well." . . . And what effect does that have?

Fred: Enlightening, really.

Commentary and Warning

A friend of mine in another state called me asking for suggestions to help a new friend of hers who had had trouble sleeping for 16 years and had become an alcoholic as a result of using alcohol daily to try to relax. I offered her quite a number of things to try, including an outline of Nick's changing tempo process. Most of the things I had suggested were not useful for her friend, so she decided to try the tempo shift. Here is her report, which she sent me a couple of weeks later.

> We did the visualizing and listening to his self-statement more slowly and with more space between the letters and words. With that, I visibly saw his body and breathing change—despite the very negative content of his self-statement. That night he slept significantly better, and he has been sleeping beautifully since then—falling asleep immediately, and sleeping 8 hours a night. He also stopped drinking on his own at the same time, and has been sober since then. He says that he never knew he could feel so good every day, and realized that he had spent the last 16 years hung over and fatigued. (T. Pepper, personal communication, 2008a)

As a result of this very brief intervention, this man made a huge change in his life, sleeping well for the first time in 16 years and stopping the daily use of alcohol. My friend wrote further:

> One of the side effects of his drinking and fatigue was that he was hyped up/manic a little bit each day, and now he isn't. Instead he is calm—and a little bored, I think—and he says he is "waiting" for his hyped-up persona to come back. I don't know if that truly is part of who he is when he is sober, or if it was purely a side effect of being alcoholic. He hasn't been sober since he was a kid, so he doesn't know the answer to that either. (T. Pepper, personal communication, 2008b)

I don't know if you notice the warning signals in this second paragraph. "'waiting' for his hyped-up persona to come back" clearly indicates a loss of a large part of his self-concept, his identity. Whenever people make a significant change that involves a loss of identity, that is much more pervasive than a change in behavior, and they need something to fill the void created by the loss. Some people can find a way to do that on their own, but others need some help. I immediately e-mailed her and warned her about this, but by then it was too late for her to do anything about it. Here is her later report:

> I agree with you about him needing to find something else to do to fill the gaps caused by stopping drinking (and all the activities he stopped in order to stay sober), but he was unable to do that. In fact, at a couple of points he went on rants about how hobbies and activities "just for fun" were a waste of time and something he had no interest in. I tried directing him toward something that would add value to his life, service-oriented activities that centered around things he already liked.
>
> Soon after that, he started to fill his time with more work, which was the only thing he felt had value. Then he ended up with 4 days off from work, and he was absolutely beside himself. His moods became unstable—very manic and hyper one minute, crashed out in bed the next. His cravings for alcohol became unmanageable, his inner critic turned way up, and it also turned against me, and some of his other housemates.
>
> It was becoming extremely stressful to be around him, and at some point I brought up a conversation about needing him to respect my things and to also speak to me respectfully without swearing at me, because both were becoming a big problem, and he went off the deep end with extreme overreaction. I was shocked by his reaction; he was nearly foaming at the mouth, shaking, screaming, swearing, turning red, and took anything I had ever said during our friendship and interpreted it as a criticism and turned it inside out as if I were his worst enemy ever.
>
> He also took every self-criticism—things no one else or I had ever criticized him for—and turned it around and accused me of thinking those terrible, demeaning things of him. He was so upset he couldn't even look at me, and I couldn't de-escalate him except by leaving. He gave me the cold shoulder for the next few days whenever I saw him, and he put in a request at work to not have any time off indefinitely. I have not spoken to him since this incident. I have run into him around town and he starts pacing, tapping his foot, and speaks extremely animated to those around him. And, of course, having run into him, I know he isn't getting the workload he was wanting, and I have heard from friends that he has been drinking heavily, blacking out, forgetting commitments. At this point, it feels too volatile for me, so for my own sanity I am staying out of his way. (T. Pepper, personal communication, 2008c)

Usually you can use the tempo shift to make a significant and useful change that will fit well with all the other aspects of your life, particularly when you do a careful congruence check before using this process. But whenever someone makes a really big change that involves a lot of his life, you need to check carefully to see if something else needs to be done. This is almost always the case with stopping the long-term use of drugs. In this case the man stopped using the drug, which involved much more than stopping the drug itself, but also all the activities involved with it—buying the drug, using it with friends, the lifestyle associated with it, and so on. But he also lost that part of his identity, which left a vacuum—"If I'm no longer an alcoholic, who am I, and what do I do?"

In retrospect, it would have been much better to change the content of this man's critical voices—the words that he said to himself—first. If that had been done, they would not have rebounded to torment him after his loss of identity, and they could have assisted him in creating a new life for himself in the vacuum created by the change.

Whenever you offer someone a change, you really need to do a congruence check to be sure the change is useful, and doesn't create as many—or more—problems than the person originally had.

Changing Tonality Directly

When you experimented earlier with changing the location, volume, or tempo of a voice and noticing how it changed its impact on you, you likely found that sometimes the tonality of the voice also changed. In the example that I gave at the beginning of this chapter, when the depressed woman changed the tempo of her internal voice, the tonality changed as well, and that was what actually changed her response. Whenever you change the tempo of an internal voice, the tonality often changes as a result, just as changing the distance of a voice almost always changes its volume.

Most of us in the United States are not very attuned to tonality, unless it is very obvious. By tonality, I mean any changes in the pitch, melody, timbre, hesitations, accent, and so on—any change in the sound of a voice other than location, volume, or tempo. In contrast, the English are very attuned to tonality, primarily because of the importance of distinguishing different social classes, which are indicated by their different regional accents. Asian languages, with their tonal aspects, require their speakers to become sensitized to fine auditory distinctions, but American English does not.

Since we tend to ignore subtle tonal patterns or shifts, much of our auditory experience is processed unconsciously, and we often react strongly to certain tones and tempos without realizing what is stirring our feelings. Sometimes I find that I am somewhat down after talking to someone, while at other times I find myself feeling quite cheerful. If I review the previous conversation, I often discover that it wasn't the content of the conversation that I was responding to, but the tone of voice that people used.

The same thing is true of the tonalities that we use when we talk to ourselves internally. If we become more sensitive to these tonal aspects of our internal voices, we can learn to change them and have more choice in how we respond.

Usually it is easier to change tonality indirectly, by changing the location, volume, or tempo, and find out if there is a spontaneous tonality shift. However, you can also try changing tonality directly, to find out if that changes your feeling response to what a troublesome voice says to you. In Nick Kemp's transcript, he asks Fred to say his sentence as if he is reading from a script and later as a question. These are two ways to change the tonality of an internal voice directly.

Unless you are a trained musician, tonal shifts are difficult to describe, because most of us don't have a good vocabulary to specify tonalities. Luckily, this isn't necessary, because all you have to do is to experiment with different tonalities and discover how they change your response, and which changes are most useful to you. One way to experiment with this is to use a different national or regional accent.

First listen to a troublesome voice and notice both the words that it says and the tonality it uses. . . .

Next, hear the same words in several different accents in turn—British, Mexican, Chinese, Norwegian, African, Russian, Italian, Swedish, Japanese, Portuguese—or any other accent that you are familiar with. Then you can try different regional U.S. accents—Southern belle, New York taxi driver, Texas drawl, New England twang, California laid back, and so on. Notice if any of those tonalities changes your response to what the voice says. . . .

Some of these accents may change your response to a voice in a way that is not useful, while others may have very little impact. But whenever you find an accent that changes your experience in a useful way, pause to think of when and where this voice is likely to speak up in the future, imagine actually being in that context, and hear it speaking with the accent you have found useful. . . .

Another way to experiment with tonality is to think of different people you know: someone who is very easily excited, and someone who is always calm; someone who is uncertain, and someone who is always very certain;, someone who is guarded and cautious, someone who willingly takes risks; someone who tends to exaggerate, someone who often minimizes; someone who often lies or only tells part of the truth, and so on. Hear the same words that your voice says in these different tones of voice, and notice if any of these change your response to what the voice says. . . .

Again, some of these tonalities may change your response in a way that is not useful, while others may have very little impact. But whenever you find a tone that changes your response to this voice in a useful way, pause to think of when and where this voice is likely to speak up in the future, imagine being in that context, and hear it speaking with the tonality you have found useful. This kind of deliberate rehearsal can make a change happen easily, automatically, and unconsciously in future situations where you want to have it. . . .

Now hear the same words in a questioning tone of voice, a commanding tone, a tone of amazement, a tone of puzzlement, or as if someone were reading the words from a written script, or any other tone that you would like to try. . . .

Again, some of these tones may change your response in a way that is not useful, while others may have very little impact. Whenever you find a tone that changes your response in a useful way, pause to think of when and where this voice is likely to speak up in the future, imagine being in that time and place, and hear it speaking with the accent you have found useful. . . .

One of the first steps in learning any discrimination is to experiment with polar opposites, or other experiences of great contrast. By beginning with noticing how we respond to the large differences in national accents, we can then gradually learn to make finer and finer discriminations, whether or not we can find words to describe them. By directing our attention to differences in tonality, we can become more and more sensitive to the tonal shifts that occur around us in everyday life. Most people ignore these subtle shifts, despite the fact that they often express very important aspects of others' state and how they are relating to you.

Up to now we have been changing different nonverbal aspects of a voice to make it less troublesome. Next we will explore how to leave a troublesome voice unchanged, but add something else to it in order to change your response to it.

3 Adding Music or a Song

Now we turn to different ways to add to your experience in order to change your response to an internal voice. A general principle is to never subtract experience; always add to it. Subtracting experience reduces your choices and abilities; adding it increases them.

Instrumental music has been used for thousands of years to elicit feeling states in people—martial music to march off to war, lullabies to help children relax and go to sleep, romantic tunes to woo a lover, and on and on.

Music is processed primarily in the right hemisphere of a right-handed person's brain, the hemisphere that does not process language, so it is less conscious, and less subject to your conscious control. If you deliberately choose to hear music internally that evokes the kind of feelings that you want to have, you can have much more influence over how you feel.

For example, Richard Wagner's "The Ride of the Valkyries" is a stirring and triumphant piece of opera music that celebrates the transportation of fallen heroes to heaven. Over half a century ago, I had a series of experiences that paired meeting a challenge—with no further time to prepare—with hearing this music played at full volume and from many unsynchronized sources. Ever since then, whenever I am facing a challenge, that music automatically begins playing in my head, creating a very positive state that supports my efforts to meet the challenge. Whatever else is going on in my life takes a backseat as I focus completely on what needs to be done in the moment.

Very early in the development of these methods, someone discovered that thinking of a problem and then adding loud circus music helped some people have a very different attitude toward the problem. Rather than being mired in their difficulty, they could think of it as if it were another stunt in a circus—something to observe with interest and excitement.

However, others who added circus music to a problem became angry, because thinking of their problem as a circus stunt seemed insulting and demeaning—it did not fit their world at all. Although changing their response from the problem state to anger showed that the music made a significant change in their response, it was not a change that was useful to them, or that they enjoyed. Adding a particular kind of music may or may not fit with someone. But if clients choose it themselves, there is a much better chance that it will be useful.

If you think about a problem that you experience fairly often getting depressed, feeling slighted by others, angry, anxious, overwhelmed, or whatever, you can ask yourself, "What kind of music would change my state in a useful way?" . . .

If you frequently get somewhat down or depressed, would a lively gypsy tune or a folk dance bring you up again? Or would a thousand violins playing a slow dirge exaggerate how you are feeling, making it seem a bit ridiculous, and less serious and overwhelming? If you experiment with different kinds of music, you can find some pieces that will be useful in changing your state in a way that is useful to you.

Mood Shift Exercise

Think of a problem mood that you slip into repeatedly and would like to have more choice about. . . .

Now think of some music that might possibly be useful to pair with this mood, and hear this music in your mind. . . .

As you continue to hear the music, think of a time when you felt this problem mood strongly, and notice what happens. . . .

Then try doing this with a different piece of music, and another, . . . until you find one that shifts your mood in a useful way. . . .

Then think of when and where this music is likely to be useful to you in the future, . . . and then imagine being in that situation, . . . and hear the music playing in your head in order to offer you more choice. . . .

Case Example: Compulsive Hand Washing

Most psychiatrists think of compulsive hand washing as a problem that is very difficult and time consuming to treat. Below is a lovely example of using a meaningful piece of music to quickly change this problem in a single brief session. This example was sent to me by Ron Soderquist, a hypnotherapist in the Los Angeles area.

> Anxious parents called, each in turn, about their 17-year-old daughter Bev, who for the past 6 months had obsessively washed her hands 3–4 hours a day. Both parents reported they had "tried everything" including counseling and drugs. They were so desperate they were now exploring hypnosis, about which they were very skeptical. Somewhat worn down by their skepticism I said to the anxious mother, "Look, because you are desperate and because you worry that once again you will be throwing money away, I will offer you a complimentary consultation. I will evaluate your daughter's symptoms and only schedule a therapy session if I believe I can help her." With this assurance, she made an appointment.
>
> As family members settled into their chairs, they all appeared relaxed. They communicated with ease, and there were no overtones of hostility. Turning to the girl, I asked about school and extracurricular activities. She immediately replied, "I have studied piano for many years and enjoy it very much." Because I play both classical and ragtime piano, this was a natural opening for building rapport.
>
> When I asked about her favorite composer, she quickly said, "Chopin." Because Chopin is also my favorite, we were now in perfect sync. We agreed we both loved Chopin's nocturnes and

we both played most of them. I asked about her favorite and she hummed the melody. I said, "When I practice a nocturne in the evening often I can hear that melody in my head all next day," and she nodded in agreement. "You can hear that melody right now, can't you?" I said. She smiled and her attention turned inward to listen, and she slipped into a nice little trance. As she did so, I ventured, "Perhaps, when you get the urge to wash your hands, you might enjoy turning on that nocturne instead." I observed her trance deepen as she considered this, and then she nodded her head and said quietly and confidently, "I can do that."

After some further rehearsal, and talk about other matters, I concluded the session. I didn't suggest another session. The mother wondered, "Do we need to make an appointment for Bev?" I looked at Bev as I said, "Perhaps she has already found a solution," and Bev nodded her head.

A week later the mother called to say Bev was doing fine. I was a little annoyed with myself for solving the problem when I should have held back and scheduled a regular appointment with a fee. But I just couldn't help myself; it was too much fun just to do it. And while there was no fee, I did get a good story, and the mother soon referred a friend.

When I followed up some months later, I asked for more details of what she experienced internally. She said that when she got stressed, she first "felt germs on my hands, and then pictured them on my hands. Then the voice in my head that said, 'You have germs on your hands. You have to wash them' went faster and louder and got more intense. When I turned on the nocturne, I would usually just hear the music, but sometimes I would imagine myself playing it." (R. Soderquist, personal communication, 2008a)

Bev had been talking to herself in a way that made her feel bad, and that bad feeling triggered her hand washing. The Chopin nocturne was powerful in eliciting a positive state in which she had no urge to wash her hands.

Note that Bev said that the words, "'You have germs on your hands. You have to wash them' went faster and louder and got more intense," which is a good indication that slowing the tempo of her internal dialogue would have been equally effective.

It is also interesting to note that nocturnes always have a very slow tempo. When she imagined playing a nocturne whenever she felt the need to wash her hands, it is likely that the slow tempo of the nocturne kept her words from speeding up and becoming intense enough to trigger the hand washing.

If Ron had added some positive words, that could have created conflict with what she was already saying to herself. However, adding instrumental music does not create conflict. Music is processed by the opposite brain hemisphere than the one used to process language, so any conflict would be between the hemispheres, rather than within one of them. Adding any music without words is a fairly safe intervention, especially if the client chooses the music that she thinks might be appropriate—and tests to be sure that it works well. Some readers might think that this example is unique, but it is actually fairly common. Ron sent me a report about another client he saw.

Case Example: Panic Attacks

> A 30-year-old male who had hung out in his bedroom for several months, couldn't drive a car etc. because of panic attacks, was brought in by his stepmother. He was too anxious to leave the back seat of his car, so I went out and started the session beside him in the back seat—a first for me! He was creating his anxiety with a habitual internal voice: "You're going to go 'weird'"—which was what he called having a panic attack. He's a guitar player, so together we found an alternate audio, a "favorite riff" that triggered his confident musician self. (I told him the Bev story while he was searching for a trigger for his confident self, and this seemed to strike a chord with him—pardon the pun.) After we practiced that for a while (I did get him into my office) he went off with his stepmother. I called the next day and he had been out hiking and feeling great, using his favorite riff to keep his musician self in charge.
> (R. Soderquist, personal communication, 2008b)

Adding a Song

So far we have been making changes only in the nonverbal aspects of your experience, without changing words. This changes your response without changing or challenging the words that a troublesome voice says. Next we are going to begin to experiment with adding words to change your experience of a troublesome voice. We will begin our experimentation with adding a song, which has both verbal and nonverbal aspects. This is a bit more complex than changing nonverbal aspects alone, because the words of the song may conflict with what the troublesome voice says. Most people have enough conflicts to begin with; we really don't want to add to that.

In the explorations that follow, be especially attentive to any response that indicates that some aspect of you objects to what you are doing, and respect that by stopping. Then you can try something a little different, and continue experimenting until you find something that no part of you objects to.

Everyone knows how a song, a jingle, a phrase, or some other auditory experience can get stuck in your head, playing endlessly, and often annoyingly. Trying to stop it is typically not effective. In fact that usually makes it stronger, because as we try to stop it, we devote even more attention to it, when what we want is to pay less attention to it.

The trick is to choose something that is more useful to you than whatever is repeating annoyingly, and a really good choice is some song that has a desired effect on your feelings. You can think of some song that has a positive effect on you, and deliberately sing it to yourself over and over, until it becomes an unconscious background music, like the mood music that is played in some stores and elevators—except that you get to choose the music.

It doesn't matter what song you choose, as long as it elicits a feeling state that you find uplifting or mood changing in a way that you like. A song is a great way to establish and maintain a mood early in the day, and it can also change your mood whenever you find yourself in a mood that you don't like.

Installing a Background Song for Mood Maintenance

Pause now to think of a troublesome mood that you have experienced repeatedly. . . .

Now think of a song that you find powerful and uplifting, and that you think could be a useful way to change this troublesome mood. . . .

Hear that song playing in your head now, and feel free to make any small adjustments in volume, tempo, and so on that increase its impact on you. . . .

As you continue to hear the song, think of a time and place when you felt this problem mood strongly, imagine actually being there, and notice what happens. . . .

Then try a different song, and then another, and another, . . . until you find one that shifts your mood in a powerful and useful way. . . .

Once you have found and practiced a song that you find useful, deliberately sing it to yourself for a while, until it becomes automatic. If you don't know the words or melody well enough to do this, find them online and practice them, so that you can. Once you have done this, all you have to do is start singing the song and it will continue on its own in the background as you turn your attention to other things. When you pause from attending to those other things, you can notice that song playing quietly in the background of your mind, maintaining your good mood.

You can also take a further step to make this connection even more automatic. If you periodically get into an unpleasant mood in certain situations, or in response to certain external cues, your can imagine being in that situation, noticing those cues. Then start the song that you have chosen, to connect it to the situation and cues, so that they automatically trigger the song. Rehearse this several times in different situations right now, and then check later to find out if it has already become automatic, or if you need to practice it some more until it does. . . .

In the earlier part of this chapter, we added music alone, but a song is usually even more powerful, because it has both words and music. Music is processed primarily in one hemisphere of your brain, while the words are understood by the other hemisphere, simultaneously activating both hemispheres with different aspects of the same message. This makes it much more powerful than either the melody or the words would be alone.

Caution

As mentioned earlier, when you add a song to your experience, its words may be in opposition to whatever you are already saying to yourself. For instance, if you have been saying to yourself something like, "Everything is going to hell," and you add the song, "I'm Sitting on Top of the World," those two messages are contradictory. This has a potential for creating conflict, and we don't want to do that.

Sometimes when I first add a song with words that are significantly different from my current mood, it seems artificial, or I have tears resulting from the conflicting moods, but often the song quickly takes over and my mood changes.

However, if you experience some discomfort, conflict, or incongruence that does not resolve quickly, please respect that, and stop what you are doing. You could experiment with choosing another song that doesn't create conflict. Or you could delay using this approach until you have learned how to add words to your experience without creating this kind of conflict. This is a major topic in many of the following chapters.

4 Talking to Yourself Positively

So far we have been experimenting with changing negative self-talk. Now it is time to explore more positive ways of talking to yourself. Even if your parents, teachers, fellow students, or others around you often talked negatively to you as you were growing up, you can learn how to talk to yourself in a more useful way. Besides making you feel better, this can support you in your activities, relationships, and goals in life.

For example, try saying the sentence, "What else can I enjoy right now?" to yourself, and notice how it changes what you attend to, and how you feel in response. . . .

That sentence directs your attention toward what you can enjoy in the present moment, rather than the complaints and problems that so often occupy our attention and make us feel bad. Even in the worst situation there is always something to enjoy, so this instruction never contradicts your reality. And it also doesn't contradict any grumpy voice that is complaining about all the nasty stuff. It doesn't oppose it by saying "but"; it just directs your attention to other aspects of your experience, saying "and," joining what a critical voice might be attending to with noticing what you can enjoy. If you say that sentence repeatedly until it becomes an unconscious mantra, it can reorient your life in a way that is both useful and enjoyable.

Contrast can often clarify and deepen your understanding of how voices work. Notice what happens if you replace the word *enjoy* with *criticize*, *disparage*, or *be disgusted by*, or some other negative word or phrase, just for a short time to notice what that is like. . . .

That kind of sentence directs your attention in a very different way, and could easily result in plenty of unhappiness, or even depression. In fact, many depressed people talk to themselves in this way without realizing it. Attending to what you don't like results in unpleasant feelings; attending to what you can enjoy results in pleasant feelings.

There is another subtle aspect of the sentence "What else can I enjoy right now?" This becomes apparent if you delete the word *else*, to get "What can I enjoy right now?" Try saying this sentence to yourself repeatedly, and notice how you feel in response, and how that is different from how you feel in response to the same sentence with *else* in it. . . .

The sentence "What can I enjoy right now?" has a very different effect, because it implies that you aren't enjoying anything right now—even though that is not a logical consequence of the statement. Most people will respond to this implication by feeling the opposite of enjoyment. When I say this sentence to myself, the tempo is slower and the tone is lower. I feel a heaviness, lethargy, somewhat depressed, because it sounds a little like a parent or teacher telling me what I should do.

The word *else* in the first question presupposes that you are already enjoying something. So you naturally feel some enjoyment—as your attention searches for something else to enjoy. What a difference a single word can make.

And of course you can replace *enjoy* with any other verb that directs your attention to what you want more of in your experience—to love, appreciate, learn, see more clearly, understand, and so on. Try saying to yourself, "What else can I love right now?" repeatedly to see how that directs your attention, and how you respond. . . .

Now pick another verb to put in the place of *love* to find out what that is like. . . .

And then do the same with *understand* or some other word, and discover what that is like. . . .

Affirmations

Many people advocate repeatedly saying positive affirmations to themselves, as a way to change their beliefs about themselves and improve their lives. Affirmations originated with Emile Coue (1857–1926) in France, who advocated saying the following sentence repeatedly, until it became an unconscious background mantra: "Every day, in every way, I'm getting better and better."

There is a very serious problem with this particular affirmation in the repeated word *every*. It will never be true that every day in every way I am getting better. Reality just isn't like that. Even if I am getting marvelously better in many ways, it won't be in every way. Most of us have an internal voice that listens for universal statements and challenges them—and those who don't have that kind of voice would be better off having one. If I say Coue's statement to myself, it stimulates my internal voice to find the exceptions to that universal generalization. It might say sarcastically, "Yeah, right! How about the way you snapped at your wife this morning—is that better? How about that sore knee that flared up yesterday, so that you're hobbling around this morning—is that better? I don't think so."

So even if the idea of affirmations might be worth pursuing, we need to be very careful about the words that we say to ourselves, or they may backfire and produce opposite results. Any universal words, like *all*, *every*, *always*, will usually stir up a protective antagonistic voice, and that may result in decreasing your optimism.

Coue's basic idea has been taken up by a very wide variety of self-help and New Age spiritual approaches and therapies. This is readily evident if you do a Web search for the term *affirmations*. Although there is no single authoritative source for what an affirmation is, there is general agreement that an affirmation is a positive sentence that you say to yourself to improve your outlook or attitude, with the goal of improving your life. (Sometimes there is an additional belief that saying an affirmation will magically bring about wealth, opportunities, or success.)

It is generally agreed that for an affirmation to be effective, it needs to be in the present tense, positive, personal, and specific, for example:

- "I am healthy, happy, wise, and free."
- "I am surrounded by people who love me."

Although "I am healthy, happy, wise, and free" satisfies the criteria above, and doesn't have a universal *all* in it, such a word is implied, and I don't know of anyone who is always healthy, happy, wise, or free. If I say this to myself when I am feeling sick, sad, stupid, or trapped, that will contradict what I experience, in the same way that a universal generalization does, so it is likely to be counterproductive.

How often is it true that you are surrounded by people who love you? You might have several people around you at home who love you very deeply, but at work or in the grocery store there are probably at least a few others surrounding you who are indifferent, and some others may even be antagonistic.

There is another problem with an affirmation that may not be immediately apparent. Some affirmations are intended to change our critical, negative self-talk—the inner chatter in which we compare ourselves to others—into something more positive.

However, saying a new affirmation doesn't magically change the old put-down voice; it just adds a new positive voice. When we introduce a new voice that is positive and supportive, conflict between it and the put-down voice is inevitable. As I have discussed previously, the old put-down voice is likely to redouble its efforts to disagree with the new positive voice. That may result in our putting ourselves down even more than we did before adding in an affirmation.

To summarize, if an affirmation is a universal statement—either explicit or implied—that doesn't fit with your reality, the part of you that keeps track of reality will be aroused to question it, defeating the purpose of the affirmation. And if an affirmation creates conflict with an existing put-down voice, that will create conflict, and often the result will be the opposite of what the affirmation was intended to do.

However, if we add an internal voice that is a bit more subtle in exactly what words it uses, there are ways around these difficulties. For example, the interesting instruction that follows was posted a couple of years ago on an e-mail newsgroup by Vikas Dikshit, an educator and trainer in Pune, India:

A Happy World

> About 18 months ago a young woman asked me for help with her depression. She was visiting a psychiatrist and had been taking some medicine for depression for the preceding few months.
>
> I suggested to her that she look around and mentally say to herself, "I am sitting on this happy chair. There is this happy table. And these are happy windows with happy curtains." I made her do this for about 10 minutes. I suggested she do this every day for about 10 or 15 minutes.
>
> After 15 days she called to say that she was feeling great now. After about 2 months she visited the psychiatrist and he stopped her medicine. She continues to call occasionally, and reports that she still feels great. The most recent one was when she was in my town about 10 days ago. (V. Dikshit, personal communication, 2007)

About a year after this e-mail, Vikas wrote that his client still felt great, and that he has used the same method—or variations of it—successfully with a number of other clients. Although this method sounds far too simple to have any effect, it employs some very subtle and powerful aspects of language.

The simplest way to understand this process is that it is the same as what all of us often do, but used in a more directed way. When someone speaks of a "cheerful fire," are they talking about the fire, or about how they feel? If someone talks about a "crappy day," they aren't really talking about the day; they are talking about their feelings. Even if the idea of happy curtains may sound a bit silly, it is really no different than talking about a crappy day or a cheerful fire, because none of those things have any emotions. When someone talks about happy curtains, that implies that the person is feeling happy.

There is usually a correspondence or equivalence between our internal state and what we perceive around us. A happy person lives in a happy world, and a sad person lives in a sad world. A sad person tends to notice sad events, while a happy person tends to notice happy things. Vikas's method uses this equivalence in the reverse direction to bring about a change in mood. Noticing happy things implies feeling happy.

Since all the sentences are about some aspect of the world being happy, there is no conflict in saying that when the person is not feeling happy. An unhappy person can still talk about happy curtains. This is very different from the "I am happy" affirmation, which will contradict your present state if you are unhappy at the time.

This process directs your attention to things around you in the present moment, just as any useful meditation does. Since you have limited attention, this will simultaneously tend to withdraw your attention from whatever you have been attending to that was making you unhappy, including any negative self-talk that has been going on in your mind.

The word *happy* is a trigger for that state, so using it tends to elicit happy feelings, no matter what it describes, even a chair or a table. When I describe the curtains as happy, that connects the word *happy* with the curtains—and with everything else around me that I describe with the word *happy*. After that, each time I look at the curtains—and the other things around me—I will tend to think of the word *happy*, and that will elicit that happy feeling. If everything around me is labeled in this way, I will soon be surrounded by things that are now associated with the word *happy*, eliciting that feeling state.

Caution

You need to be very cautious if you include other people or animals in your happy statements, because that may create a contrast that is not helpful. If I notice a happy child, that may make me feel happy, because I am not a child—just as I am not a chair or a curtain. But if I notice other adults being happy, that contrast with my present state may make my unhappiness worse. So it is much safer not to include other people or animals at all, and just notice inanimate objects.

Another way of thinking about this method is that it is an example of the hypnotic language pattern called *selectional restriction*. Since a window can't be happy, your mind will unconsciously attempt to make meaning out of the word *happy* by applying it to something else. If you are alone, you are the only other available possibility, and even if you are with others, you are still a possibility. Since other people and animals can be happy, there is no need to apply happiness to yourself in order to understand the sentence—another reason not to include other people and animals. All this processing will usually occur completely unconsciously, so it can't be countered by your conscious thinking.

Of course, despite all these wonderful understandings, this process can be completely nullified if someone uses a voice tone that is sarcastic, scornful, or depressed, as we explored in Chapter 2. But if you use a tone that is ordinary, simply reporting your experience "objectively," or a tone that indicates even a little bit of pleasure, it will work very nicely. Whether you do this with yourself or with someone else, you can notice the tonality, and change it if it does not support the process.

Using the Method for Other Outcomes

You can also use this method with any other useful adjective, such as *calm* or *peaceful* for someone who is too easily agitated, *loving* for someone who feels angry, or *balanced* or *centered* for someone who feels scattered or chaotic. Simply identify the problem mood or feeling, think of its opposite, and then select an adjective that expresses this opposite mood to put in the place of *happy*.

For instance, if someone is often fearful or anxious, the opposite of that is safe, and they can use this word to describe the world around them. "I see the safe chair," "Those are safe curtains," "This is a safe computer," and so on.

Be sure that you choose an opposite experience, not a feeling in the midrange of a continuum. For instance, if you are often critical and rejecting, the opposite of that would be a feeling of *welcoming*, *loving*, or *embracing*,—not *accepting*, which is too neutral.

Think of an unpleasant state that you sometimes slip into. . . .

Then think of its opposite, a positive feeling state that you would like to have in its place. . . .

Then use this word to describe or comment on the things around you. You can do this either internally, or out loud. Continue to do this for several minutes, and notice how it changes your feelings. . . .

This method is an affirmation that will work, and that won't arouse other conflicting voices to disagree with it. What can we learn from the two examples I have offered you: "I am sitting on this happy chair," and "What else can I enjoy right now?"

Four Principles of a Useful Affirmation

1. It directs your attention to events in the present moment, withdrawing your attention from whatever is going on in your mind that may be contributing to your unpleasant state.
2. It is a process that you can do right now—whatever your present state is—in contrast to an end point (enjoyment, happiness) that may seem unattainable and distant in time.
3. It doesn't contradict your reality in the moment.
4. It directs your attention to something in the world external to you, in a way that naturally and indirectly elicits an internal resourceful state of enjoyment, happiness, and such.

These four characteristics of a positive affirmation that works can be put to use for other states. Let's take the other three qualities in one of the previous examples of an ordinary affirmation: "healthy, wise, and free." How could you use the models given above to elicit a feeling of being healthy? . . .

- "I am sitting on a healthy chair," and so on.
- "What else can I notice about my healthy functioning right now?"

Now do the same with *wise* and *free*, and then go on to create affirmations about pleasure, beauty, love, balance, or whatever you want more of in your life.

- "What else pleases me right now?"
- "What else is beautiful to me right now?"
- "What else can I love right now?"
- "What else is balanced in my experience right now?"

Another exercise that Vikas offers to participants in his trainings is provided below.

Appreciate and Smile Exercise

> With their eyes closed, I ask clients to imagine they are standing in front of the front door of their home. I ask them to feel the key in their hands and hear it turning in the lock as they open the door. And then I ask them to appreciate the door, and smile. . . . Then I ask them go around the home and appreciate and smile at everything that they see or hear. . . .
>
> And then repeat the same process of appreciating and smiling with all the family members, neighbors, and acquaintances. . . .
>
> And then do the same for the other places that they visit often, like office, school, or shops. . . .
>
> And then repeat this with some strangers as well. . . .
>
> And I also ask them to go inside their own bodies and appreciate and smile with all their body parts. . . .
>
> The whole exercise takes about 15 minutes when I teach it; it requires less than 15 minutes when people do it on their own. I suggest that they do this every day for about a month or so, and notice the results.
>
> Once again, the idea is to connect that appreciative and smiling state to all the usual things and people in the person's life. It does not paste a fake smile on their face; it increases the chances that the person will generally appreciate and smile and be happy everywhere. (V. Dikshit, personal communication, 2008)

Paul Ekman's (2004) excellent and detailed research has shown that even if you ask people to smile artificially—or simply hold a pencil between their teeth, which requires the same kind of muscle movements around the mouth—it tends to elicits happiness because that muscle position is unconsciously associated with smiling, and smiling is associated with pleasure and happiness.

Vikas's instruction is more subtle than asking someone to deliberately smile. It first asks you to see something externally, and then to say some words of appreciation internally, creating a natural context for a spontaneous smile.

In this chapter I have presented a number of ways that you can talk to yourself without contradicting what you might already be saying to yourself. They are elegant and graceful ways to change your experience that you can do consciously, despite the fact that they work in a way that is largely unconscious.

Next we will explore how to replace an existing voice with a new voice that is more useful. We have to be very cautious when doing this because there is always a potential for conflict.

5 Adding a Voice

In previous chapters you have learned how to change nonverbal aspects of the direction, location, volume, tonality, and tempo of a troublesome voice in order to reduce its impact on you. You have also learned how to add music or a song to a voice in order to change your response, and in Chapter 4 you have experimented with several ways to talk to yourself positively that are useful and effective.

Now we can begin to use some of these methods in combination to make a useful change. For instance, if you first reduce the volume of a troublesome voice, you can then replace it with a more resourceful and supportive voice without creating significant conflict. The following is another example from Ron Soderquist (2008d).

Bill's Critical Voices

> A middle aged woman called to say she wanted her husband to come in for hypnosis to change his attitude. "I am sick and tired of his negative attitude." I was amused, and asked her to have him call me. She was right. When Bill came in for an appointment he said, "I grew up in a very negative, unhappy family. There were no 'Atta boys' in our family; there was only criticism. They were unhappy with their marriage, and it was a rare day when Dad or Mom laughed or showed happiness." He went on, "My wife complains that I come home from work grumbling and complaining. She says I'm just like my parents, and she's probably right, but I can't seem to help myself. I don't see how you can help me change. I don't like being so angry with the kids, and I don't like having an unhappy wife. If you can help me change, great."
>
> After some questioning, Bill identified his parents' negative voices in his head. I asked if he could imagine a room in his head with the voices coming from a radio or some device over by the wall. He was able to imagine a radio. Then I wondered whether he would like to go over and turn down the volume, or perhaps put a pillow in front of the radio to muffle the sound. As he did this, he gave a big sigh, and visibly relaxed. "What's going on?" I asked.
>
> "My head is quiet for the first time ever," Bill said. I told him, "Since it's your head, you can put in anything you want. For example, because you are thankful for your family and your health, you can fill that room with your own thankful voice, if you wish." To his surprise Bill discovered he could do that quite easily. We rehearsed him in reviewing his thankful thoughts while driving home from work, so that he could greet his wife and children with joyful energy. After some rehearsal, he felt confident he had installed new voices in his head. Bill's wife called later to report she was enjoying a new, positive Bill; he had changed his attitude. (R. Soderquist, personal communication, 2008d)

I think it is pretty amazing that you can change a pervasive, lifelong negative attitude in a few minutes, just by changing an internal voice—without extensive therapeutic time traveling back to the traumatic historic origin of the voice.

However, I want you to think about what might have happened if Bill hadn't reduced the volume of his negative self-talk before adding a resourceful and supportive voice. If there were two loud voices in his head, they would conflict with each other, setting up an internal battle.

Ongoing Internal Conflicts

Many people seek help because they already have chronic unpleasant internal conflicts. A common troubling conflict is between some version of "Be sure to do what others approve of," and "No, be independent and think for yourself." A conflict like this often puts you between a rock and a hard place, because whatever you decide to do, afterward the other side will torment you. "You just went along with the crowd again, you wimp," or "You sure blew it with the guests by telling that racy joke."

Another common kind of conflict is between indulging in a present pleasure on one hand and its future consequences on the other. One voice may say something like, "Go ahead and treat yourself to that dessert; you deserve it," while another warns, "If you eat that, you'll get fat, and no one will want to be around you." Whether or not you eat the dessert, the other side will badger you with the consequences later. "You denied yourself a simple pleasure that would have made you feel really good," or "Now you've done it; you'll have to watch what you eat all next week to lose the calories in that cheesecake."

Talking Back to a Critical Internal Voice

A number of widely respected therapies—and most books about negative self-talk—strongly advocate talking back to a critical internal voice as a way to lessen its influence. For instance, David Burns is a student of Aaron Beck, who is sometimes described as the father of cognitive therapy or cognitive-behavioral therapy (CBT) (Beck, 1987). CBT has even deeper roots in the work of Albert Ellis, whose work was originally called Rational Therapy, later Rational-Emotive Therapy, and finally Rational-Emotive Behavior Therapy, as it evolved over the years (Ellis, 2007). As early as the 1950s—over half a century ago—Ellis advocated actively verbally challenging a client's self-defeating beliefs and behaviors by demonstrating the irrationality, self-defeatism, and rigidity of negative self-talk. Burns is one of many cognitive therapists who advocate countering a troublesome voice in this way:

> ***Talk back to that internal critic! . . .***
>
> a. Train yourself to recognize and write down the self-critical thoughts as they go through your mind;
>
> b. Learn why these thoughts are distorted; and
>
> c. Practice talking back to them so as to develop a more realistic self-evaluation system. (Burns, 1999, p. 62)

In this process the client is taught how to notice the content of *automatic thoughts*, identify the kind of *distortion*, and then generate a *rational response*. For instance, if the automatic thought is "I never do anything right," the distortion is overgeneralization, and a rational response is, "Nonsense, I do a lot of things right."

"This shows what a jerk I am" is an example of the distortion called labeling, and a rational response is, "Come on, now, I'm not a jerk."

These rational responses disagree with and oppose the troublesome voice. Other people don't like being disagreed with, and internal voices are no different; they are likely to become defensive and redouble their efforts to convince you of what they are saying.

Burns developed this method while working with seriously depressed patients who were often suicidal, having given up all hope of having a normal, satisfying life. The main symptoms of depression are feelings of hopelessness, helplessness, and worthlessness. Most—if not all—depression is in response to internal voices that criticize, berate, and torment. In this context, rallying patients to oppose their internal voices can be a huge step forward, and research indicates that CBT gets results with depression that are superior to those of antidepressant medication and most other therapies.

Since then, Burns has applied the same method to quite a variety of other problems that result from troublesome internal voices, including anger, guilt, addiction to love and approval, and perfectionism. If someone who is suffering from one of these problems feels completely hopeless and helpless, then mobilizing a rational response to the internal self-talk that elicits these feelings can be a very useful first step in dealing with the conflict, but not the end goal of integration and resolution.

Although a battle between two voices might be somewhat better than only being a slave to a troublesome voice, it is still an inelegant solution that leaves the person split between the two. It is much better to reduce the impact of the troublesome voice before adding a resourceful voice.

The Positive Outcome of a Negative Voice

Reducing the intensity of a troublesome voice is only useful if the voice has no positive function or intent in the present. There is at least a possibility that a troublesome voice might have some useful information for you. Often an internal voice wants to protect you from some kind of problem or danger, even if this is hidden inside insults and criticism. It could be warning of an actual physical danger: "If you did that, you could get seriously hurt." Or it might caution you against being disappointed, embarrassed, or criticized by others—dangers to your social status, or your idea of who you are. "Don't make a fool of yourself at the party tonight."

Often a voice once had a useful function in a past context, but it is now outdated and irrelevant. For instance, a voice may once have warned you not to anger Dad; now that Dad has been dead for years, it no longer serves a useful function, so it can be safely reduced in volume. But at other times a voice wants you to notice a mistake, so that you can improve what you do. "Boy, you really screwed up that interview!" What a voice says may be unpleasant, and may even be counterproductive, but it usually has the positive intent of making your life better in some way.

If you just reduced the volume of this voice, you would also lose its useful positive intent—throwing out the baby with the bathwater. Many people desperately need some kind of warning voice, because they keep making the same mistakes over and over without noticing. Losing a protective voice can have consequences that are much more unpleasant than feeling bad.

Bill's voice was apparently simply a result of his history with his critical and unhappy parents. Since it had no useful function in the present, its volume could be reduced without losing anything. But when a voice still has a positive function, simply reducing the intensity won't work well, and the voice is likely to stay loud or return. Although reducing the volume of a troublesome voice reduces potential conflict, it doesn't eliminate it altogether, so even this solution is not as elegant as it could be, and I explore other more elegant alternatives in later chapters.

Here is another nice example of adding a more resourceful voice to a troubling one, again from Ron Soderquist.

Case Example: Tommy Bangs His Head

The mother, Julie, called me and related: "Our Tommy is 5 years old and we are worried about him."

"What does he do that worries you?"

"Whenever he spills milk at the table or makes any mistake, he gets out of his chair and bangs his head against the wall while saying, 'You are stupid. You are dumb.'" I invited them to come in as a family.

It appeared that the parents were a normal couple. There were no "red flags" in their relationship with Tommy. Nor was there anything of note in Tommy's body language. Julie reported that her son enjoyed kindergarten and played well with friends. He had no other strange behaviors. However, Tommy would bang his head a few times a week on average. This behavior had been going on for at least several months.

I first considered recommending testing for autism. But in my experience, behaviors can often be addressed by simple, self-hypnotic suggestions. I looked directly into Tommy's eyes, and began telling a story. . . .

"Once upon a time there was a little boy squirrel named Timmy who felt bad because he couldn't do anything right." Tommy nodded his head. "When Timmy climbed trees with his friends he would slip and fall down." Tommy nodded his head again. "When Timmy hid nuts he would forget where he hid them. He felt dumb." Tommy nodded his head again. I embellished the story in great detail so Tommy would fully identify with Timmy the squirrel.

"Timmy the Squirrel's parents finally brought their little boy to visit the Wise Old Owl who lives in the big oak tree. Because owls have wonderful eyesight he saw them coming from afar, and said, 'I see you are a squirrel family. How can I help you?' Mommy and Daddy told the owl that Timmy banged his head against trees and called himself names when he made a mistake.

"The Wise Old Owl thought for a moment, and then he looked right at little Timmy and said, 'Little Timmy the Squirrel, do you have a belly button? Let me see your belly button.'" At this command, Tommy pulled up his shirt and looked at his belly button.

"The Wise Old Owl continued, 'Little Timmy, take a good look at your belly button, because everyone who has a belly button makes mistakes. From now on, whenever you make a mistake, just look at your belly button and say: It's OK. Everyone who has a belly button makes mistakes.'"

Then I told him, "Now you and your Mommy and Daddy go home and enjoy being part of a loving family." At that, I ended the session. Julie called the following week to report Tommy had stopped banging his head (Soderquist, personal communication, 2008e).

Like the previous example of Bill, the man with a critical attitude, Tommy's voice apparently had no positive function in the present. Some of the things that we learn are pretty much random. Tommy may have heard something like his voice at school, or on the playground—kids can sometimes be even more cruel and unthinking than adults—and somehow it stuck with him as something very important. All he needed was some skillful instruction in how to think differently. In this case, the instruction was embedded in a story about a squirrel, and Tommy's nodding and looking at his belly button clearly indicated that he fully identified with Timmy the squirrel.

I'd like to point out the importance of telling Tommy to look at his belly button, something that could easily be overlooked. If

Ron had just said, "Everyone makes mistakes," it wouldn't have had nearly as much impact, because it would be too abstract and general, and not tied to any specific cues to trigger it. It might not necessarily apply to Tommy, and he might not remember it at the appropriate times. Having him look at his belly button provides a specific visual cue that both triggers the thought and applies the generalization to him specifically. Every time Tommy looks at his belly button—or imagines seeing his belly button—he will think of the instruction, "It's OK. Everyone who has a belly button makes mistakes." The visual cue will trigger the thought many time a day, even when he has not just made a mistake.

Another way of thinking about what Ron did with Tommy is that he taught him a way to be more self-accepting. Making mistakes is something that everyone does. Recognizing that something is a normal thing to do is a process that is often called *normalization*. Let's follow up by exploring self-acceptance in more detail.

Self-Acceptance

Whenever someone doesn't like something about themselves, they are likely to criticize and reject themselves, which is the opposite of self-acceptance. Then if they learn about affirmations, they may try saying something like, "I deeply and completely accept myself." That sets up a direct conflict between the self-rejection and the self-acceptance, as I have discussed earlier.

However, there is an accepting way to talk to yourself that doesn't conflict with any self-rejection that you already experience, and I'd like you to experience what that is like.

First think of something that you don't like about yourself—your weight, your getting angry, not speaking up for yourself, dark moods, or whatever it might be. . . .

Then listen to what you say to yourself when you think of this. "You're a fat lazy pig," "I get angry all the time," "You're a wimp," "I'm no fun to be around," or something like that. . . .

Now try saying to yourself, "I deeply and completely accept myself," and notice what you experience in response to that. . . .

There are a variety of ways to respond to this, but what they have in common is some kind of weakening of the self-affirmation, because of the conflict between the two sentences.

Linking Apparent Opposites

Now try putting your two sentences together in the following way, beginning the sentence with "Even though":

"Even though I [am a fat lazy pig, get angry, am a wimp, have dark moods, etc.], I deeply and completely accept myself."

Say that sentence several times, and notice how you feel in

response, and how that is different from what you experienced when the two sentences were separated. . . .

The words "even though" have a very interesting way of joining what seem to be opposite or contradictory experiences. After all, not liking something about yourself is certainly the opposite of deeply and completely accepting yourself. "Even though" completely accepts your not liking something and joins it with deep and complete self-acceptance. It states the opposites in such a way that they don't conflict with each other, integrating the two.

This exact sentence "Even though I [critical self-evaluation], I deeply and completely accept myself" is used in a method called Emotional Freedom Technique and also appears less prominently in other approaches. However, "even though" can be used in many other ways to join apparent opposites.

- "Even though I have failed repeatedly, I can learn to succeed."
- "Even though I don't like healthy food, I can lose weight."
- "Even though I'm lazy, I can satisfy my boss."

The general pattern is the following:

> Even though I [statement of problem or difficulty], I [statement of a positive outcome].

Try this yourself. First think of a personal lack, or something about you that you criticize, and then think of a future goal or outcome—to be happier, calmer, smarter, more perceptive, or something else, and link them together using the sentence above. Notice how you experience that. . . .

Linking the Present to the Future

There is another value in doing this that may not be immediately apparent. When people criticize themselves, they often use sentences to link their problem or lack to a future failure or inability:

- "I have failed repeatedly, so I can't succeed."
- "I don't like healthy food, so I can't lose weight."
- "I'm lazy, so I can't satisfy my boss."

Think of some sentence like this that you say to yourself, and then restate it in the form "Even though I [statement of problem or difficulty], I [statement of a positive outcome]," and experience what that is like. . . .

That kind of sentence links a problem to an outcome in a very interesting way that is the opposite of what most people usually do. It is almost as if you are saying that the problem will make it easier to reach your outcome.

- "Because I have failed repeatedly, I'll be able to succeed."
- "Since I don't like healthy food, I'll be able to lose weight."
- "Being lazy will make it easier to satisfy my boss."

Even though those sentences may seem totally crazy to you at first, try saying them to yourself as if they were true, and then think about how they actually could be true. . . .

Here are just a few realizations—out of many other possibilities:

- "Failing repeatedly means that I know a lot about how to fail; if I just do the opposite, that should be a path to success."
- "Some healthy food is fattening, so avoiding that will make it easier for me to lose weight."
- "Since I'm lazy, I'm motivated to find ways to get a job done faster with less effort, and that will make my boss happy."
- "When I think that a sentence is totally crazy, thinking how it could be true can sometimes result in a useful new understanding."
- "Even though this may be new to you, you'll find yourself noticing when you and other people use the words "even though," and become more aware of the change in attitude and outlook that results from doing that."

Since adding a more useful voice can be so dramatically helpful, what would happen if we added several of them, speaking simultaneously, like a chorus? In the next chapter I explore how to do that.

6 Auditory Perspective

The word *perspective* may seem out of place in a book about internal voices, because that word is usually understood visually, as a way of seeing events, or a particular point of view. The word perspective is often used in an abstract or metaphorical way, in contrast to a specific description or instruction about what to do. If someone has ever told you, "I wish you could get a better perspective on this problem," you probably had no idea how to accomplish that—even if it sounded like a good idea to you. The person speaking to you provided a general outcome, but no specific way to actually achieve it, something that is often true when people give advice—or do psychotherapy. *

Visual Perspective in the Moment

There are many different kinds of perspective, and it can help to first illustrate them in the visual system, where they are more familiar and easier to describe, before moving to the auditory system.

Fundamentally, the word *perspective* is used in situations in which we experience something in relation to something else, the "the appearance of things relative to one another." This is something that we do unconsciously thousands of times a day, because it is important to know how things around us are related to each other. If I want to pick up something that is lying on a table, I need to know its location in relation to me in order to do that.

In a painting, when we see similar objects (such as trees) painted in different sizes, we don't see them in isolation; we see them in relation to each other. Because of our experience of things in the real world, we perceive the smaller ones as being farther away, creating a sense of distance and depth, even though the painting is actually flat. If a painting showed a mouse and a person the same size, since we know that a mouse is actually much smaller than a person, we would either see the mouse as much closer to us to account for this, or assume that the mouse was much larger than normal, a giant mouse.

The Larger Context Creates Perspective

One way to describe most problems or unhappiness is that we develop tunnel vision, narrowly focusing on a problem while ignoring everything else that surrounds it. Expanding our field of vision to include much more of what is happening simultaneously in the moment provides a larger context that is literally wider and broader in scope, in which we see the problem in relation to what is around it, the "big picture" that includes much more information.

---

* This chapter is adapted from the appendix to Andreas, S. (2002). *Transforming your self: Becoming who you want to be.* Boulder, CO: Real People Press.

For instance, if you have a plumbing problem, and you focus on that alone, it can seem overwhelming. You may even go on to other responses, like, "Oh, it's not fair; these things happen at the most inconvenient times," a line of thinking that takes you into an unpleasant and unfair world of experience—and away from your problem entirely. But if you expand your focus to include all the other aspects of your home that are functioning well to keep you warm and safe, or think about what it would be like to have no plumbing at all, you can put the plumbing problem in perspective by relating it to other things or events that could have happened to you, but didn't.

When seen in a larger context, a problem typically appears much smaller and easier to solve. The additional information included in the big picture may even provide a basis for a solution that wasn't available when you focused exclusively on the problem. If you have ever had a bad leak in a pipe and tried to stop it, expanding your scope to include the main shutoff valve helps tremendously.

Years ago I had a friend who often focused very narrowly. Once we were working together on a truck, putting on a radiator hose. He was busily tightening the metal clamp with a screwdriver, and he was puzzled because the hose was still loose, even after he had been tightening it for some time. Finally the hose started folding and crumpling, and he realized that it had slipped off the metal tube at the back of the radiator. He was so focused on the hose and the clamp that he didn't notice something very obvious that was only a few inches away. On another occasion, he was using a pocketknife to cut a string that bound together a bunch of fruit trees that we were going to plant. He was oblivious to the fact that he was holding the bundle of trees with his left hand; as soon as the knife cut through the string, it would go right into his hand. When I alerted him to this, he moved his hand.

When a doctor has to tell someone bad news about a serious illness, he or she typically only talks about the problem and what needs to be done. The person receiving the bad news will usually think of the illness in isolation, and may become very upset. Besides feeling terrible, the resulting stress doesn't help patients make difficult decisions about treatment alternatives, and also doesn't help them heal.

Now imagine that your doctor did the following, instead: "If we were to take CAT scans or MRIs of your entire body, and put them up on view [gesturing as if putting a series of a dozen or more images up on a translucent viewing screen], we would find that almost all of them would show that your body is functioning in a healthy way, responding quickly and appropriately to any temporary injury or imbalance. Now [putting up one more image] there is a significant problem in this one area that we need to do something about."

Seeing the scan of the illness or injury in relation to all those other (imaginary) images of healthy functioning would create a much broader perspective in which the illness would seem much less significant and less upsetting, and the prospects for treatment and recovery would seem much better.

Perspective Across Space and Time

Another kind of perspective is to see an event that occurred in one place and time in relation to another in a different place and time. If someone you care for scowls at you, it would be easy to assume that he is angry with you and become upset. However, if you remember that he lost his job a couple of days ago, you can view his unhappiness in relation to that past event, and perhaps feel some compassion for what he is going through, a very different response that will probably be more useful than getting upset. When you create this kind of perspective, you connect the image of the scowl and the memory of the job loss, creating a simultaneous representation of the two events together.

Whenever we plan, we think of what we can do now, in relation to how it will influence what will happen later, in a sequence of experiences. "If I leave before 3, I'll avoid rush hour traffic." "If I prepare thoroughly, then I'll be pleased with the result." "If I turn down that sweet dessert now, I'll be able to enjoy a slender body that feels good all the time." This connects two different images in a sequence in which one follows the other, perhaps with a little arrow to indicate cause and effect. Another way to do this is to create a short time-lapse movie of this kind of connection.

A Perspective With Multiple Positives

Yet another kind of perspective results from seeing an unpleasant event while simultaneously seeing several pleasant ones. For instance, you can literally see someone's annoying behavior side by side with several images of times when you enjoyed that person's companionship in different ways. Seeing all those positive images together with the unpleasant one at the same time provides a balanced perspective that would be lost if you only saw the annoying behavior in isolation.

A Perspective Movie

We also tend to take a problem experience out of the flow of time. If you see a still picture of a problem event, it isolates it from all the events that preceded it and all those that followed it. And since a still picture doesn't change, it seems to last for all eternity, magnifying the unpleasantness. It is easy to feel stuck in the unpleasant feelings that result. This is something that often happens in people who have post-traumatic stress disorder or other traumatic memories. While this kind of concentration can sometimes be useful in studying a problem to see what can be done, a narrow view often leaves out the very information that we need in order to start moving toward a solution.

When you see a friend or partner doing a behavior that particularly annoys you, if the behavior is a still picture that fills your field of vision, you have lost perspective in this way. If you allow that still picture to expand into a movie that includes what happened before and what will happen later, you will likely find many, many pleasant events. When you see that annoying habit embedded in the flow of all the events in this larger time span, it typically seems much less important, less upsetting, and much easier either to accept or to start working toward a solution.

To summarize, we can gain perspective by seeing an event in relation to its larger context in the moment, in relation to some other future or past event, or in the larger flow of events that occurred before and after that event. We can gain exactly the same kind of perspective in the auditory system.

For instance, if someone makes a critical comment, and it occupies all your attention, it can be pretty devastating. But if you also recall all the complimentary things that the same person said to you both before and after the critical comment, that expansion of your time frame can put that one comment in perspective auditorily. That makes it much easier to hear the critical comment and then consider whether it is something that you can use for feedback. It might be very accurate information about your behavior that is important to be aware of and do something about—even if it is communicated poorly. Or it might be only information about the speaker's frustration so it really has very little to do with you, and you can safely ignore it.

Auditory Perspective

We often focus our "tunnel hearing" on one voice while ignoring the tone of voice, other voices, or all the other background sounds. You can broaden your scope of hearing to include all these sounds around you to provide a larger auditory context: the "big sound" that can create the same kind of perspective as the "big picture."

You can relate what someone says in one place and time to something at another place and time, either from the past to the present, or from the present into the future. Recalling what someone said long ago may be useful to you in the present, or may be helpful in forecasting what someone may say in the future. You may decide to refuse something that a small child wants, saying, "No, you can't have that," and hope to hear later, "Thanks, Mom, I'm so glad that you were firm with me; that saved me a lot of trouble."

Hearing one voice surrounded by a number of others will be familiar to anyone who has listened to a chorus singing. Although usually those in a chorus sing the same words, sometimes with different melodies, some choral works interweave different words as well as different melodies. This creates the same kind of perspective in the auditory system as seeing one image surrounded by others does in the visual system. And since this is something that many people have not learned to do, it can provide a particularly powerful new way of gaining perspective about a troublesome negative voice. This kind of auditory perspective has been developed by John McWhirter, a consultant, therapist, and trainer who has an approach he calls Developmental Behavioral Modelling.

Auditory Perspective Demonstration Transcript

Steve Andreas: I'd like to demonstrate one way to gain perspective with a troubling voice in the auditory system, using a process I learned years ago from John McWhirter. I don't need to know any content. It can be your own voice, or someone else's voice, or it could even be a sound that has no words with it. (Tim volunteers.) Tim, first I want you to listen to that voice, and verify that it still makes you uncomfortable. . . .

Tim (looking up, and then down left and frowning): Yes, it sure does.

Steve: It looks like you get a picture first, before you hear the voice. Is that right?

Tim: Yes.

Steve: That's fine. We can still use the voice. Is this your voice or someone else's?

Tim: It's my voice.

Steve: OK, so you're talking to yourself. Where do you hear the voice?

Tim: Behind my head, to the right a little.

Steve: OK. Now just let that voice go to wherever voices go when you're not listening to them, and think of four times in your life when your own voice served as a strong positive resource to you, perhaps commenting on a job well done, or saying "You can do it," or some other support. Think of them one by one, and listen to what each one has to say, and the tonality, until you have four of them. . . . (Tim nods.)

Steve: Now position those four voices around your head, more or less evenly spaced, wherever seems appropriate to you—perhaps one in front, one in back, and one on either side, leaving an empty space at the back and right, where you heard that troubling voice. When you hear those four voices all talking at once, it will be harder to hear the details of what they are saying, but you can still hear the tonalities, and know the general nature of what they are saying. Let me know when that is set up, with all four voices talking at the same time, kind of like a chorus with different parts. . . . (Tim nods.)

Steve: OK. Now bring that troubling voice back in to join the other four, and listen to all five voices at once. Notice if this changes your response to that voice in any way. . . .

Tim: It's farther away now, and not as loud. I feel better; it's easier to listen to it. I can hear some of what it's saying as useful information, while before I was just noticing my bad feelings.

Steve: OK. Great. Does anyone have any questions for Tim?

Tess: Were you able to understand what the five voices were saying when they were all talking at once?

Tim: No. I knew they were there, and I could pick out bits and pieces, and the meaning was there, but I couldn't really hear all five voices at once.

Steve: That's typical of most of us, and it's important to warn people about this, or they may think that they aren't doing the process correctly. I met a woman once who was born blind and only got her sight when she was about 30. She could keep track of eight different speakers simultaneously, as if she had an eight-track tape recorder. But very few people can do that, and it's not necessary for this process to work.

Tim: When I had the four resource voices talking at once, I felt like I was sitting in a big, comfortable overstuffed easy chair, as if the voices were literally supporting me physically.

Steve: That's a nice spontaneous synesthesia; you experienced the positive voices as a kinesthetic feeling of support.

When all five voices are being heard simultaneously, the four resource voices provide an auditory background perspective for really hearing the problem voice, instead of just being overwhelmed by the bad feelings that it generates when it is heard alone. Some people think of this as "The four resource voices are overpowering the problem voice," or some other description that presupposes conflict or competition, but that is a less useful way of understanding this process. The resource voices are not in disagreement about one event, saying "but." They are simply all speaking at the same time about different events, saying "and," providing a more balanced perspective.

If the original troubling voice had been someone else's voice, I would have asked Tim to choose four voices of other people. The reason for making sure that the resource voices and the troubling voice are all either your own or someone else's is to avoid creating any possible conflict between your own views and someone else's. For instance, if the troubling voice were your own, and the resource voices were someone else's, it would be easy to think, "They may disagree with me, but I know better," or some other conflict like that. As much as possible, we want to make changes that avoid creating any additional conflict.

Auditory Perspective Process Outline

Now you can do the same process that Tim did. Ideally you would do this with another person, so that one of you can read the directions, and the other can relax and devote complete attention to following the directions.

After one person has done the process, you can switch roles so that you can both experience it. Many people find it much easier to attend to their inner experience if they close their eyes while doing the process. But if it is easier for you to do it with your eyes open, that is fine.

1. **Choose a voice.** Think of a troubling voice, and notice your feeling response to what it says. . . . Notice the location of the voice, and whether it's your own voice or someone else's. . . . Then set that voice aside temporarily.
2. **Remember positive voices.** Recall four resource voices, times when you (or someone else) commented favorably about something that you had just done, or said something else supportive. If the problem voice is another person's, the resource voices should also be someone else's; if the problem voice is your own voice, the resource voices should also be yours. Listen to each voice in turn, noticing both the words and the tonality, and how you feel in response to hearing it. . . .
3. **Arrange voices.** Position these voices around your head—leaving a space for the location of the troubling voice—so that you can hear all four voices talking at once. It will be harder to hear the details when they are all talking, but you will still be able to hear the tonalities, and have a sense of the meanings. . . .
4. **Bring in the troubling voice.** Allow the troubling voice to return to its location, and listen to all five voices talking at once. . . .
5. **Notice your response.** Notice how your feeling response changes in either intensity or quality, or both. . . .
6. **Test.** A few minutes later—or longer—you can check to find out how well the change has lasted. Simply recall the troubling voice, and notice your response to it. Find out if your response is still different than it was before going through the auditory perspective process. Typically the change will last without doing anything else. Whenever you hear the troubling voice, you will again have the more comfortable feelings that you had when you first heard all five voices together.

When the change resulting from this method doesn't last, you may need to repeat the process using voices from different times and places. If you do this several times without success, usually it indicates that some other important outcome is served by continuing to be distressed by the troubling voice. For instance, being upset by the voice could be useful in getting a spouse to assist you in some way, or to avoid some unpleasant task or duty. In that case, you need to find some other way to get assistance or some other effective behaviors to use to avoid the task. Sometimes that is as simple as learning to say, "Honey, I want some help here," or "No, I don't want to do that," instead of using your bad feelings to influence others around you.

There is nothing special about using four supportive voices; it is a nice number that works well. But you could also use three, or you could use more, and these additional choices might work better for certain people. Using three would make it easier to hear the details of the voices; hearing five or more could strengthen the chorus, even though the details of what they say would be harder to hear.

Next I explore some additional useful ways of talking to yourself at the beginning of the day, so that you can start your day in a good state. If you start the day well, it is much easier to maintain a good state in the face of later unpleasant events. That is much easier than starting off badly and then having to work to change it.

7 Starting Your Day

Some people bounce out of bed in the morning, eager to start the day, while others keep hitting the snooze button on their alarm, and then struggle to slowly drag themselves out of bed. The way you start the day is likely to set the pace for the rest of your day. If you start out eager and animated, it will be much easier to maintain that state, despite any difficulties that may occur later. But if you start the day discouraged, or in some other unpleasant mood, then you will have to work yourself out of that state in order to feel better, which is usually much more difficult.*

What often makes the difference is what you first say to yourself as you emerge from sleep. You may awaken in response to an alarm clock, or in response to light, or to the sounds of others in the house getting up. As you begin to waken and sense the world around you, what are the first words in your mind? What was the first thing that you said to yourself this morning? . . .

How about yesterday morning? . . .

Now check several other recent mornings. What did you say then, and how did it set a tone for the rest of the day? . . .

* This chapter was adapted from pp. 13–16 of Andreas, S. (2006). *Six blind elephants: Understanding ourselves and others*, Vol. 2. Boulder, CO: Real People Press.

Now notice all the tonal qualities of that internal voice—the tone, volume, tempo, hesitations, and so on. . . .

If you said something like, "Ohmigod, I have to go to work today," in a discouraging tone, you probably had to work hard to get out of bed and get going, and that attitude is likely to persist during the rest of the day.

On the other hand, if you said something like, "Wow, which of my projects do I get to do first?" in an enthusiastic tone, then getting out of bed was probably very easy, and it would take a really unpleasant event to change your positive attitude.

Programming Your Morning

If you would like to change how you talk to yourself in the morning, there are six simple steps:

1. **Desired outcome.** First, think about how you would like to feel as you start out your day. . . .
2. **Desired self-talk.** What words could you say (or sing) to yourself, and what tone and tempo of voice could you use to create that feeling? . . .
3. **Identify cues.** Next notice what you will see, hear, or feel as you first begin to wake up, and then say (or sing) those words to yourself. . . .

4. **Check for objections.** Notice any objections or feelings of concern that you might have about doing this. . . .
5. **Satisfy objections.** If you have any objections, identify any problems with either the words that you chose, or their tonality and tempo. Then adjust what you say (or sing) to yourself, or how you say it (or both) until any objections or concerns are satisfied. When all aspects of you are satisfied with it, it will be something that you are congruent about wanting, and it should occur spontaneously and dependably. . . .
6. **Rehearse and test.** Imagine waking up in the future in order to test what you have done. Experience what it will be like tomorrow morning, when you first begin to realize that you are waking up, and notice what happens. . . .

If your morning sentence occurs automatically, you are done. If it doesn't, you may need to rehearse it several more times just as you begin to wake up to make it automatic, or you might have to back up a few steps and adjust what you say to yourself, or the tonality that you use.

Next I want to offer you a somewhat more complex way to begin the day, one that can be used to change a wide variety of problems, as well as achieving positive outcomes.

Behaving "As If"

Giorgio Nardone and Claudette Portelli, in their book, *Knowing Through Changing*, use the following instruction as part of their work with clients. It's a very interesting method that can be used to change any problem whatsoever, by installing an internal voice that initiates a daily pattern of thinking and behavior.

> During the following weeks, I'd like you to ask yourself this question. Every day, in the morning, question yourself: "What would I do differently today if I no longer had my problem, or if I had recovered from my problem?" Among all the things that come to your mind, choose the smallest, most minimal but concrete thing, and put it into practice. Every day, choose a small but concrete thing as if you had already overcome your problem, and voluntarily put it into practice. Every day choose something different. (Nardone & Portelli, 2005, p. 73)

Before reading further, pause and reread the instruction above, perhaps several times, so that you can remember it. Then think of a problem that you have, and vividly imagine actually carrying out this instruction tomorrow morning. . . .

Then imagine doing it the next morning. . . .

And then imagine doing it for several more mornings over a period of a week or so. . . .

Then review your experience, and notice how this instruction redirected your attention, and how you responded to that. . . .

This instruction is an example of tasking or homework, in which someone is given specific instructions about what to do outside the therapy session to create or support a desired change. Many of Milton Erickson's interventions directed clients to do certain things that would change how they experienced their problems. Often these instructions were puzzling and mysterious, and often they were delivered within a hypnotic trance in order to amplify their impact and to make sure that they were carried out.

Erickson often talked about making a small change that would begin a snowball effect, growing into a much larger and more lasting change. However, this certainly isn't true of all our attempts to change. We often make a small change and it doesn't snowball at all. We may make some effort, resolution, or decision, and then quickly backslide into our old behavior. What is the difference between a small change that will snowball in a useful way, and one that won't? There are many different elements in this instruction that support each other and that result in a cascade of change.

Elements of the Method

"What would I do differently today if I no longer had my problem, or if I had recovered from my problem?" is a very interesting instruction. It uses an "as if" or pretend categorization—that the client has recovered from the problem—to create a make believe world in which anything can happen, free of the constraints and limitations of the real world. This neutralizes any objections based on judgments that someone might have about the instructions being impossible, unrealistic, silly, stupid, and so on. It also changes your attention from the problem to the solution—what it would be like to have recovered from the problem.

Within this make-believe world, you are asked, "What would I do differently?" This question focuses your attention on what you can actively do that is different from what you have been doing—in contrast to passively hoping for some change to come magically from a therapist or someone else. This focuses your attention repeatedly on the solution, rather than the problem—and this will be true even if you don't actually do any of the things that you think of.

The phrase "Among all the things that come to your mind" presupposes that many things will come to mind, focusing attention on all the things you would do differently if your problem was solved.

The instruction "Choose the smallest, most minimal but concrete thing, and put it into practice" appears to make the task easy, minimizing any residual reluctance. However, in order to choose the smallest thing, you have to think of all the things you have thought of. Thinking of "all these things" strengthens each individual thing by associating it with all the others. If you had been told, "Just pick one thing you would do differently," you wouldn't have to think of all of them. The instruction to choose the smallest thing seems to minimize the task, but it actually makes it more impactful, because it draws your attention to all the things you would do that were different.

The "as if" frame links the phrase "What would I do differently" with "if I no longer had my problem, or if I had recovered from my problem." Then when you actually do one of the concrete behaviors, that makes it real, taking it out of the "as if" categorization. Since this real behavior is linked with recovery, that implies that it is equally real that the problem has already been overcome. Usually this will occur entirely outside of your conscious awareness; you will only notice that your life is going better, or that your problem is somewhat better.

Another way of describing this is that every morning you think about having recovered from the problem, and then do a specific behavior that validates the implied recovery. Since every morning begins with the implication of having recovered from the problem, that makes it likely that you will also think of it, consciously or unconsciously, at other times throughout the day. This instruction would not be nearly as effective if it were assigned in the evening—unless perhaps there was an explicit suggestion to continue to do it in your dreams while sleeping.

You are to choose the "smallest, most minimal" thing to do, in order to make the task appear easy. However, it really doesn't matter how small the task is; it will still create the connection between the "small thing" done, and recovery. If a smile is an indication of happiness, it doesn't matter how small or brief it is.

Since you do this over a period of weeks, and each morning you have to choose a different smallest thing that you would do if you had recovered, each day you will have to choose a somewhat larger thing from the remaining ones that you have thought of.

If you enlarge the list by including additional smaller things that would indicate recovery, that means that you will think of the solution even more often as you review this larger category of things in order to choose the smallest one. And if you are at all oppositional or rebellious, you may decide to do one of the larger things, giving you an opportunity to resist a little, while still complying with the overall task. If you do a larger thing, that will be even better evidence for the implication that you have recovered.

Furthermore, since each morning you do something different in the category "what I would do if I had recovered," soon there will be a group of things that you have already done that indicate that you have recovered. That group of experiences will become larger and more compelling each day, providing more and stronger evidence for having recovered as time goes by.

Thinking of the actions that indicate recovery and doing one of them each day will also sensitize you to when you do these actions spontaneously during the day. For instance, if smiling or laughing are two of the behaviors, and you find yourself smiling or laughing sometime during the day, you will tend to notice that you have spontaneously smiled or laughed, instead of ignoring it. A spontaneous response is even better evidence that you are recovering than a deliberate action.

And if you refuse to do the task, you will probably still think of it every morning, perhaps even more than if you did it. Even thinking of the task will sensitize you to all the behaviors that would indicate that you have recovered from the problem. This inner rehearsal will make it more likely that you will do one (or more) of the behaviors, and will also make it more likely that you will notice them when they occur spontaneously.

This instruction is a beautiful example of how to pack a host of implications and presuppositions into a task, most of which will be completely outside the person's awareness. This instruction will work just as well when you understand its structure, and you can also give the instructions to yourself, rather than being told by someone else.

Using this Method Generatively

The instructions can be made more generative by rewording them so that they are not about a problem, but about a positive outcome that would expand your resourcefulness, creativity, enjoyment, and so on. Pick some positive outcome, a change that you would like to make, and then ask yourself, "What would I do differently today if I had my outcome?" . . .

For instance, let's say your outcome is to have a better relationship with your partner. Each morning, think about all the things that you would do if that were already true. Would you speak in a softer tone of voice? Would you listen longer, even when what she is saying isn't that interesting to you, or you have heard it many times before? Would you touch her gently when you ask for something? Would you think more often about her desires, or what she would find enjoyable? Pause now to pick a positive outcome, and then think of a number of things that you would do if it were already achieved. . . .

Each day, choose the smallest of the things that you think of, and actually do it. Each day choose a different thing to do. You will soon find out what a useful and effective task it is.

Nardone and Portelli developed their intervention out of a theoretical and practical orientation that can generally be described as a strategic approach, which is significantly different from the one in this book. Although they don't have the same background, their instructions include a number of fundamental principles, while missing some others.

The first and most obvious missing piece is the lack of an explicit process to develop a well-formed outcome, in order to make sure that the outcome will actually accomplish what you want. I describe a detailed process for doing this in Chapter 9.

The other major omission is the lack of any explicit congruence check to be sure that reaching the outcome will preserve the person's other desired outcomes. Even a simple question like, "Does any part of you have any objection to doing any of these things?" would begin to explore how a proposed solution could have drawbacks or problems that would impede or block reaching it.

Nardone and Portelli have successfully used this pattern with a variety of eating disorders, obsessions and compulsions, and depression—all significant problems that are often quite difficult to treat. In all of those problems, the behaviors are pretty commonplace, so I think it is unlikely that someone would set an outcome that would cause serious problems.

However, if this intervention were to be applied to an outcome like flying an airplane, or gaining some other skill that could put the person or someone else in danger, congruence could become a serious issue; hopefully this would be taken care of in a careful outcome specification process that preceded the instruction.

General Versus Specific Interventions

This intervention is a very general one, with wide applicability (any problem), so of course there is a corresponding lack of precision. Some fundamental interventions like rapport, or a solution focus, are a useful part of resolving a wide variety of problems. More specific and detailed interventions will usually be much more effective with some problems or outcomes, and much less effective with others that have a different structure.

My favorite example of this is that a phobia has the exact opposite structure from grief. In a phobia someone steps into and reexperiences a very unpleasant memory, while in grief, someone steps out of a very pleasant memory (Andreas & Andreas, 1989). If someone were to try to use the phobia cure on grief (or the grief process on a phobia), it would make the problem worse, not better. That is why my preference is to use very specific and detailed interventions that are precisely designed to do exactly what someone wants—or what someone needs, which is not always the same. As more and more detailed specific patterns for specific problems or outcomes are developed, this becomes even more true.

However, any process that works is worth learning, and the instruction above is a wonderful example. One of its great advantages is that the instruction is complete in itself, and does not require any special skills on the part of the person using it. The process can even be given in written form, as I have done here, so that people can try it on their own.

In this chapter I have reviewed some additional ways to add a voice to your experience in order to make a useful change. Next I want to explore a number of very important aspects of the words that we use to describe our experience.

8 Generalizations, Evaluations, Presuppositions, & Deletions

Negative self-talk has many different aspects. Usually it describes events or ourselves in ways that make us feel bad. However, it can do this in a variety of ways, some of which are somewhat hidden, and difficult for most people to detect. Among them are generalizations, evaluations, presuppositions, and deletions. When you know how to detect them, it is relatively easy to adjust your communication accordingly, and avoid the significant dangers they sometimes pose.

Generalizations

Words are one of the primary ways that we generalize about our experience, a very useful skill. When someone uses the word *chair* we know immediately that is something that we can sit on.

However, this skill also has some very serious drawbacks. For instance, notice what specific image comes to your mind when you read the word *chair* in the previous sentence. What kind of chair is it? What does it look like? What shape is it, what color? What is it made of? Is it new or old, and so on? . . .

Do you suppose that the image of your chair looks the same as the one that I had in mind when I wrote the previous paragraph? Mine was a hotel meeting room chair, with shiny chromium metal legs and frame, and some gray-blue coarse cloth upholstery.

Yours was probably different from mine in a number of ways. Often we think of a somewhat generic chair, perhaps a wooden dinner chair, or some other common type of chair that you might find in a home. Or you might have thought of a particular chair that is special or familiar to you in some way. You probably didn't think of a lawn chair, a throne, or an antique chair.

When we use a single word like *chair* to describe a wide range of things that we can sit on, that is a very useful way to organize our experience and communicate at least a rough idea of it to someone else. We know that something described with the word *chair* can be used in a certain way, roughly what size it is, and something about what it is made of, how long it is likely to last, and so on. For contrast, compare your image of the word *chair* with your image of the word *cloud* or *mountain*, and you can begin to notice how much information a single word can indicate.

When we identify several different objects as a chair, we tend to think of what a chair can be used for, and ignore all the differences between individual chairs. And we also do something else; we tend to forget that a chair can be used for many other purposes than sitting—to block a door, to impress the neighbors, to fend off a snarling dog, and so on. In many areas of our lives this only occasionally causes some misunderstanding. You may offer to give me a chair, and I accept, thinking of an ordinary chair. But when you arrive with your museum piece chair, I realize that it wouldn't fit in with any of the other furniture that I have.

Prototype

The image that comes to your mind when you understand a word is called a *prototype* by cognitive linguists (Lakoff, 1987). When we hear or see a word like *chair*, we use our prototype to represent all the objects that could be described as a chair, and then we respond to this prototype image, because this is what gives us the meaning of the word. This usually is not a significant problem when we are thinking of a chair, or some other physical object, though it can be. For instance, if someone offers me a "drink," I may accept, thinking of water, while my host may have alcohol, strong coffee, or something else very different in mind.

This kind of misunderstanding is often much more problematic when we describe events that are judgments about each other or ourselves. For instance, when we describe what someone just said about us as a *criticism*, that word—just like the word *chair*—can describe and evoke a multitude of experiences that we have had throughout a long period of time and in a wide range of situations. What image will we use as a prototype to represent and understand the meaning of that word?

Often we will use an emotionally charged memory of what someone said when criticizing us in the past. If we do, then we will respond to that image, rather than to the present event. Another way of responding to someone's else's criticism is to internally hear a loud chorus of many criticisms that we have experienced over a period of years. The present event might be a very small criticism about how we did the dishes. But our emotional response may seem all out of proportion to others unless they realize that we are responding to vivid images from our past.

This process often occurs below the level of our conscious awareness, so we may not even realize that we are responding to these past events instead of the present. We may only notice the horrible feelings that we have as a result.

As soon as we have labeled what someone said as a criticism, we are likely to forget that the same utterance could be labeled as a comment, feedback, honesty, good information, caring concern, or some other description that would evoke a very different prototype image, and a very different feeling response. This is one of the many ways that words can trap us in unpleasantness. Using a different word to describe the same experience, or set of experiences, elicits a new meaning that can release us from that trap.

Quite often we have the experience of receiving messages of appreciation or caring from many people in a row, followed by one message that is critical or rejecting. What do we typically do? Most of us ignore the many appreciations and caring that we received, and feel bad about the one rejection. We may even dismiss all the positive comments with a wave of the hand that shoves those images aside, often actually saying something like, "That's irrelevant" or "Those don't count." This is using our ability to generalize in a way that is not useful, and all of us find ourselves doing this at times.

"A Bad Day"

It is common for someone to say, "I had a bad day," which can be very discouraging—especially if we have several in a row. But what does "having a bad day" really mean? Occasionally we may have a day in which it seems as if everything goes badly all through the day, from dawn to dusk. But almost always the truth is very different—that we had one, two, or possibly even several things go badly, and we generalized from those to the entire day, when actually the rest of the day went rather well. Saying that we had a bad day ignores all the things that went well, distorting and contaminating our experience, and making us feel much worse than we really need to. John McWhirter has developed a very simple process for reevaluating this kind of destructive overgeneralization.

Decontamination Pattern

Use this pattern for overgeneralized experiences that contaminate all the details with the summary feeling. For instance, "a bad night out" contaminates all the good things that someone might have experienced during that period of time. The overgeneralization also tends to ignore the specific bad events, so they are not attended to in detail, and are difficult to learn from. The sentences in quotes below are the instructions for the process:

1. "Think of the bad event, for example a bad night out, bad interview, bad day, and so on." . . .
2. "Now think of what was particularly bad in this event. This may temporarily result in your feeling worse." . . .
3. "Now notice that there are lots of things that are neutral, not directly involved with the particular bad event." (Pause to let the person search for examples.) . . . Then you can suggest additional examples, which will extend the range of examples and move the person's attention further away from the specific bad event. "For example, the feeling in the back of your knee, the colors of what you see, other sounds that you hear, and so on." . . .
4. Now continue to notice what else is involved in that whole situation, and notice that there are aspects that would have been enjoyable had you not been distracted by the unpleasant event. For example, the sound of birds outside, other people around, enjoyable memories that you could think about, positive possibilities that you could be exploring, all the many things you could have been enjoying had you not been distracted by the unpleasant event." . . . The suggestions given are first directed to what actually happened

> within the event and then extended to memories, thoughts and images that you could have attended to in that situation; there are always positive thoughts you could be thinking.
>
> 5. "Thinking about the whole situation, how would you summarize it now?" . . .
>
> Usually the situation is now experienced in a much more balanced way. The same process can also be very useful for overly positive generalizations, because specific negative events are ignored and not available to learn from. (J. McWhirter, personal communication, 2007)

When we describe ourselves, our ability to generalize can cause even more trouble, particularly if people describe themselves as a loser, a failure, or some other similar word. Take a moment to think of what the word *loser* means to you. . . .

What prototype image did you use to understand that word? . . .

My image of a loser is not just someone who has lost a race, or a job, or a girlfriend. It is of a stubble-faced disoriented homeless person in rags, who has lost almost everything. If I describe myself as a loser, the prototype image that I think of is likely to be a huge distortion of who I actually am. And my emotional response to my image of myself as a loser is likely to be way out of proportion to what actually happened, the loss of a job or a relationship.

When I use a word like *loser* to generalize about myself in response to a specific event, such as losing a job, that word tends to spread through all of space and time—I am a loser in all situations, throughout all the past and on into the future. That is what is often called overgeneralization, but in fact all our generalizations—no matter how useful—are overgeneralizations.

Using the word *loser* also makes it very difficult to think of all the times in my life when I have succeeded at something. Those other images of successes could bring some perspective to thinking about my loss, and elicit a more resourceful emotional response, but thinking of myself as a loser prevents that.

Universal Words

When we use universal all-or-none words like *all* or *always*—or *none* or *never*—our generalizations become even more explicitly universal. "I always lose." "I never say the right thing." "None of the things I do will ever succeed." When people generalize into the future in this way, I usually ask them to show me their fortune-telling license. Usually they look a bit puzzled, until I point out that they are predicting the future without being adequately trained and certified.

A single word or phrase like *loser* can carry a very heavy load of meaning and affect us very strongly—whether someone else says it, or we use it to describe ourselves. What does it mean to say that someone is a loser? It may mean that someone has little financial ability or poor social skills, or some other lack.

However, using the word *loser* generalizes that to all of that person's life, when that is never the case. Someone who is described as a loser may have little money or status, while having many good friends, a wonderful sense of humor, a beautiful voice, and so on. Using the word *loser* ignores all that, making it seem as if the person has lost in all aspects of life, not only now, but throughout the past and future.

Applications of the Decontamination Pattern

McWhirter's pattern described above can also be used for any unpleasant overgeneralization about the self. "You're no good." "I can't do anything right." And it can also be used for any positive overgeneralizations that could also use some balance. Just as retrieving the pleasant aspects of a negative generalization can make them available for learning, retrieving the unpleasant aspects of a positive generalization can do the same.

These are just a few of the many traps that lie in wait for us when we use words, because except for proper nouns like "Bill Smith," every word is a name for a generalization. Every generalization is an overgeneralization that has these potential drawbacks (Andreas, 2006).

Evaluations

When we generalize about events, the words we use may be simply descriptive generalizations, like *chair*, *small*, or *new*. However, usually a word also expresses some kind of evaluation. A word like *small* may carry a meaning of "insignificant" or "unimportant," and *new* often carries a meaning of "better." Many other words, like *stupid*, *lazy*, or *worthless*, express much more obvious negative evaluations.

If an internal voice were to say, "I think you're stupid," that might be unpleasant, but it is clearly stated as an opinion that someone else has about you; it is not necessarily a fact. Since it is clearly someone else's evaluation, if you have a different view of the behavior or event that was labeled as stupid, you can offer it.

A sentence like "I think you're stupid" usually ignores the context. Someone could be very stupid in one context, and quite intelligent in another, but when the context is omitted, the statement appears to be universal—that you are stupid everywhere and all the time.

However, it is much more common for an internal voice to say, "You're stupid," a statement of a fact rather than an opinion about a fact. That makes it much less clear that it is an evaluation that someone else has made about you. One way to clarify this is to reply, "OK, you think I'm stupid; what events or evidence convinced you that this is true?" That can begin to unravel what otherwise appears to be an undisputable fact.

If an internal voice says, "I'm stupid," instead of "You're stupid," the evaluation sounds even more like a fact. Whenever the self is describing itself, that creates a tight circularity that is a bit more difficult to disentangle. While occasionally people may come to a conclusion about themselves on their own, usually it is an echo of what they heard someone else say. They accepted it, and began to describe themselves in that way. Since they agree with it, it is much harder to think of alternative descriptions.

Unraveling Evaluations

As I pointed out in an earlier chapter, one way to begin to unravel a statement that someone makes about himself is to change it into a statement that someone else makes about him. "Look, I'm sure that you didn't pop into this world saying this to yourself. When you were an infant, you didn't even understand words, much less talk to yourself—you had to learn that much later from other people around you. You may have learned to say this to yourself, but it is really what someone else said to you, so it is much more accurate to say 'You're stupid' than 'I'm stupid.'"

After this first step of opening up the circular self-referring statement, you can follow up with, "Who said this to you?" making it clear not only that it is someone else's opinion, but whose opinion it is. That provides a context for the statement, because who says it has a bearing on its truth and importance. "What kind of person is saying this?" Then you can go on to ask about the larger context: "Where were you? What just happened?" and so on. Thinking of all these circumstances that led to the conclusion that you were stupid offers many opportunities to spontaneously reevaluate the conclusion, and think of alternative meanings.

Utilizing Self-Reference

Another way to unravel someone's troublesome self-statement is to realize that the evaluation describes itself, so it applies to itself. If the self is stupid, then the statement itself must also be stupid. "OK, if I'm stupid, then saying, 'I'm stupid' must be stupid." If a voice says, "I'm a worthless person," that statement must itself be worthless. "I'm lazy" is a lazy statement, and "I'm insensitive" must be an insensitive thing to say. Most people don't notice this circularity, but when you point it out, it is hard to deny.

This circularity will apply to anything that people say about themselves. Try this now with any negative statement that you say about yourself. Think of some general critical statement that you say about yourself, and then turn it back on itself in this way, and you can have an experience of this. . . .

When any negative self-referring statement is applied to itself, it tends to nullify itself; it becomes much weaker, and so will your feeling response to it. Interestingly, this circularity has a very different effect when used with positive descriptions. If I say, "I'm intelligent," then logically that must be an intelligent thing to say. It might not be true, but at least it is consistent; the statement doesn't nullify itself (Andreas, 2006).

Presuppositions

In everyday life, we presuppose a great deal. In writing this book I presuppose that you can read English, and that the words I write will be meaningful to you. Whenever we use pronouns like *he* or *she*, we presuppose that a listener will be able to fill in the blank with the appropriate person. If I say, "I couldn't find the cat," that presupposes an I, a cat, and that I have been searching for the cat. These ordinary presuppositions rarely cause trouble.

However, when an internal voice says something like, "I can't believe how stupid I am," stupidity is no longer an opinion, it becomes a presupposed fact. That makes it much harder to recognize that it is actually still an opinion. Even when you change that to a statement that someone else makes—"I can't believe how stupid you are"—it is still a presupposed fact. There are many other ways to disguise an opinion as a fact by presupposing it. Here are just a few:

- "If you were to become smart, I would be very surprised."
- "It was your stupidity that caused the problem."
- "If you were smart, that wouldn't have happened."
- "It's amazing how stupid you are."

One way to recognize presuppositions would be to learn how to recognize the 31 linguistic forms that can be used to create a presupposition (Bandler & Grinder, 1975). That can be very useful for anyone who works therapeutically with other people. But fortunately there is a much easier way to detect presuppositions: Take any sentence and negate it, and notice what is still true.

For instance, if I negate the first sentence above, that yields, "If you were to become smart, I wouldn't be very surprised." The presupposition that you are not smart is still intact. Try negating the other sentences above, and you will find that the presupposed stupidity is still there in each of them. . . .

Of course the same linguistic structures can be used to deliver presuppositions that are more positive and useful. If you say to a child, "I can't believe how smart you are," or, "It would surprise me if you became stupid," you can presuppose the child's intelligence, making it much more likely that the child will accept that as a fact. Try substituting any positive word for *stupid* in the sentences above to confirm that this is true. . . .

Deletions

Ordinary sentences omit a lot of detail in order to be short and efficient. I may say, "I don't want to go," which deletes both the destination and how I would go there if I went. I assume that the listener will know this and will be able to fill it in from the preceding communication or the context. I may say, "He gave it to her," which doesn't tell you who the people are or what was given. Again, usually the larger context tells you what the pronouns *he*, *it*, and *her* stand for. Someone might say, "I like this better," which doesn't specify what "this" is, or what she is comparing it to. In ordinary conversation this process usually works quite well, but it can also sometimes lead to confusing—or amusing—miscommunications when the listener fills in a deletion with the wrong image.

When we talk to ourselves, we use the same kind of deletions and pronouns, often without the larger context that would give them a complete and detailed meaning. When we talk to ourselves negatively, this can lead to serious misunderstanding and a great deal of suffering.

"You're Not Good Enough"

For instance, one woman would say to herself, "You're not good enough," and break out in tears. Her mother had never actually said these words to her, but she had often offered advice on how to do things differently or better. The mother's positive intention in doing this was to help her daughter learn and develop her full capacities as a young woman. However, the daughter had concluded from this that she was never good enough, a huge overgeneralization that had tortured her with insecurity and doubt for decades.

My intervention was very simple: I laughingly pointed out that what she was saying to herself had no object—"Good enough for what?" "Are you good enough to drive a car, good enough to speak intelligently, good enough to write a letter, good enough to go to a grocery store?" She spent the whole time driving home, and much of the next week, saying to herself, "I'm good enough to—" and then laughingly filling in the blank with something else that she was clearly good enough to do, including some things that were amusing to her, like, "I'm good enough to be in a rodeo." This built a new generalization about herself based on all the ways that she was good enough, balancing the old generalization that had tortured her for so long.

In the same way, someone who tortures herself by thinking, "I have to be better" can ask herself to supply the missing "better than what?" A workaholic who says, "I have to work harder" can ask himself, "harder than what?" Someone who describes herself as "a loser" can ask herself to enumerate exactly what she has lost—as well as what she still has.

Think now of something that you say to yourself, and identify any deletions. . . .

Then ask yourself a question directed to what is missing, and ask it over and over again to build a new generalization, to create some balance in this aspect of your life. . . .

We really can't avoid using any of these different aspects of language, but when we understand how they work, we can examine any troublesome communication and modify it so that it becomes less troublesome.

In the next chapter I examine one of the most difficult and confusing aspects of language, negation, and its much more useful opposite, positives. We will learn how to change negative statements into positive outcomes, a path that can lead you easily from what you don't want to what you do want.

9 Negative Messages & Positive Outcomes

Negative Messages

The word *negative* has at least two very different important meanings. One of these is equivalent to "unpleasant" or "I don't like it." For instance, if someone said, "You're ugly," and you would like people to think you are good looking, you would probably think of that as a negative comment. However, someone else who thinks that good-looking people are shallow and vain might think of that as positive. This use of the word *negative* depends on the values of the person making the judgment.

There is another quite different use of the word *negative* that is much more specific and unambiguous, namely that a statement contains a negation. For instance, a word like *not*, *none*, or *never* (not ever) clearly indicates negation. Another form of negation is a prefix like un- im- or in- that means "not," as in unmanageable, imprecise, or incompetent.

The sentence "You're ugly" may be unpleasant, but it does not contain a negation. However, the sentence "You're not good looking" has a negation in the word *not*. Most people would say that those two sentences mean the same thing, but people actually experience them in ways that are subtly but significantly different. Try saying, "I'm ugly" and then "I'm not good looking" in turn, and pay close attention to what image you use to represent the meaning of each sentence in your mind. . . .

If you don't immediately notice the difference, alternate between the two sentences while you notice the images that you use. . . .

Reversing the negation in the two sentences above offers another experience of contrast that can sensitize you to how negation works. Change "I'm ugly" to "I'm not ugly," and then change "I'm not good looking" to "I'm good looking," and notice how you respond differently. . . .

When you hear a sentence with a negation, a very curious thing happens; you represent whatever is negated, and then that image is canceled, erased, or crossed out in some way. Even though that image is canceled, it is in your mind briefly, which draws your attention to it, and that tends to influence your behavior.

The familiar example "Don't think of pink elephants" is a communication that elicits exactly what the command tells you not to do. It is self-contradictory, and no one who understands English can read that sentence and not think of pink elephants. Now that you are thinking of pink elephants, try not to think of them, and notice what you experience in response to doing this. . . .

Most people experience an internal struggle between thinking of them and trying not to think of them. When someone does this, even more attention is devoted to the struggle between these two urges than was devoted to the original pink elephants alone.

Thinking of pink elephants is relatively innocuous, and won't lead to any behavior, except perhaps annoyance or amusement. However, if you think of some action or response, like not eating a fattening food, or not feeling nervous, your images of eating and feeling nervous will tend to elicit those behaviors. Even though they are negated, those images will be in your mind, creating an urge, and the negation creates a conflict that draws your attention even more to what you don't want to do.

For instance, many people who have weight problems have an internal voice that repeatedly reminds them not to eat, contributing heavily to the problem. If people who want to lose weight say to themselves, "Don't think about that delicious chocolate cake in the refrigerator," that will direct their attention in a way that is likely to result in their eating the cake and gaining weight, which is what they don't want. When they discover this internal voice and realize how it contributes to their problem, usually their first response is to want to get rid of the voice, which is another negation.

It really isn't possible to get rid of a voice. And even if you were able to stop an internal voice, that would leave an empty space. Our senses and our thoughts don't like to be idle, so something else would likely soon fill this space, and it might be something even more troublesome than the voice you stopped.

Although trying to stop something in your mind is self-defeating, deliberately replacing it with something else is relatively easy. If you think of something you would rather think of, like orange kangaroos, or agile aardvarks, the pink elephants will simply fade away into the background of your attention—until I mention this, and you notice that you are not noticing them, bringing them into the focus of your attention again.

All of us sometimes talk to ourselves in negations that are not useful. For instance, it is common for someone who is about to have an interview or make a public presentation to think, "Don't get nervous," or "Don't choke up." Those sentences direct attention to an image of being nervous or of choking up, and those images will tend to elicit exactly the feelings and behavior that we don't want.

Whenever you discover yourself using negation in this way, you can refocus attention on something more positive that will redirect your attention. If you are getting ready for a public presentation, you can say to yourself, "Stay calm," or "I wonder how much calmer I can be," and if you want to lose weight you can say something like, "Eating well will lead to my being slender and feeling better."

The other main alternative is to utilize negation in a more positive way by saying something like, "Don't be too calm when you prepare to speak," or "Don't think about how great you will feel when you have reached your desired weight." That kind of self-talk uses negation to direct your attention in a much more positive and useful way (Andreas, 2006).

Negation is very tricky process, particularly when our statements apply to ourselves, rather than only our behavior. For instance, thinking, "I am not a cruel person," will not work well, but "I am a kind person" will. In general, it is much better to avoid using negation.

However, even attending to a positive statement of what you want can sometimes be tricky. For instance, some people want to have self-worth or self-confidence, and that sounds like something positive. However, if people feel a lack of self-worth, that is actually a negation of who they are. Then if they try to gain self-worth, that will be an attempt to negate the original negation, creating further conflict. It usually works much better to identify the original negation of self-worth and change that to something more positive (Andreas, 2002).

To summarize, if you are aiming an arrow at a target, it is much more useful to attend to where you do want the arrow to go than where you don't want it to go. It is much more useful to talk to yourself so that you attend to what you do want than what you don't want, much more useful to attend to a solution than a problem. Attending to a positive desired outcome rather than a negated problem is a very important first step.

Getting What You Really Want

However, the next step is to make sure that what you say to yourself will actually get the results that you want. Every culture has some folk tale like W. W. Jacobs's *The Monkey's Paw*, in which someone is given three wishes. In these stories the last wish is always used to undo the damage caused by the first two. For instance, in one such tale, a hungry peasant couple are given three wishes. Since she is hungry, she immediately wishes for a salami. He is enraged that she would wish for such a trivial thing, and wishes for the salami to grow onto her nose. Then the last wish is used to remove the salami from her nose, and they are right back where they started—still hungry, but hopefully a bit wiser about what is worth wishing for. There are many other sayings with the same message of caution.

- "There are two great tragedies in life; one is to not get your heart's desire; the other is to get it." (George Bernard Shaw *"Man and Superman" [1903], act 4*)
- "Remember that not getting what you want is sometimes a stroke of good luck." (H. Jackson Browne, *The Complete Life's Little Instruction Book,* p. 222. Nashville, TN: Rutledge Hill Press, 1997.)

- "Being frustrated is disagreeable, but the real disasters in life begin when you get what you want." (Irving Kristol, *On the Democratic Idea in America*, p. 31. New York, NY: Harper 1973.)

If you specify your outcome carefully in advance, you can avoid these gloomy prophecies. Fortunately there is a systematic way to examine any desired outcome and modify it to be reasonably sure that it will be satisfying.

Positive Outcomes

A well-specified outcome will work effortlessly and unconsciously, while avoiding objections, hesitations, and obstacles. To be well formed, an outcome has to satisfy certain conditions. One of the main conditions is that it does not interfere with or prevent other outcomes or desires that you have. The only way to discover that is to specify your outcome in sufficient detail that you discover very clearly how it might affect other areas of your life.

The first thing to realize is that every change—no matter how wonderful it is—will result in some loss. That loss may be trivial, or it may be vitally important to you, but there will always be a downside. For instance, if you move to a much nicer home, that change in location may mean that you are farther from a favorite delicatessen, or closer to a noisy freeway, or it may mean that you are continually worried or stressed by a longer commute or a larger financial obligation. Knowing that there will always be a downside to every change can alert you to search for what it is, so that you can examine it carefully in advance and not be surprised later. Once you have examined the consequences carefully, you can either be prepared for them or change your desired outcome to avoid them.

There are a number of other criteria for an outcome that will be achievable and satisfying. You can use the questions and statements in the outline below to examine any outcome by asking someone else (or yourself) the questions in italics. Continue to ask each question until you are satisfied that it has been answered fully, and that you know exactly what the answers mean. In the following, I use public speaking—which some studies identify as something that most people fear more than death—as an example of an outcome.

Outcome Specification Outline

In the following, the sentences in italics are the therapist's instructions.

1. **Desired state.**
   a. *"What do you want?"* "I want to speak in public without choking up and forgetting what I want to say."

b. *"State the outcome in positive terms"*—what you do want, not what you don't want. "I want to feel comfortable speaking in public, easily able to recall what I want to say."
c. *"Is this initiated and controlled by you?"* (No magic intervention by someone or something else that is out of your control, like winning the lottery.) "No matter what the situation, I'll be able to maintain a comfortable state, as if I were speaking to a close friend, or a small group of friends."
d. *"Give me a specific sensory-based description, and/or give me a behavioral demonstration of what you want."* Specify it so that someone else would know exactly what you want. "I want to feel just like I do now while speaking to you. I'll be breathing normally, feeling alert and able to remember what I want to say, and speak clearly and convincingly." (This kind of sensory-based description or behavioral demonstration will be a criterion for all the other conditions listed below.)
e. *"Give me an example of what you want."* Choose an appropriate scope. "I want to feel comfortable when speaking in meetings of about 10 people." (Not "I want to be comfortable in all situations.")
f. Meta-outcome (see step 9). *"When you have that, what will that do/get for you?"* "I'll have the satisfaction of making my views known to others, and be able to affect the group decision in useful ways."

2. Evidence procedure: appropriate and timely feedback.

a. *"How will you know when you have it? What specific evidence will let you know that you have achieved it?"* "I'll be able to feel comfortable, easily recall what I want to say, and speak clearly."
b. *"What specific evidence will let you know that you are making progress toward your goal?"* "I'll see the other people attending to what I say, and their questions will usually indicate that they have understood what I said."

3. Context.

a. *"Where, when, and with whom do you want it?"* "I also want to be able to present information to a larger group of a hundred of my colleagues at national conferences."
b. *"What specific sensory-based cues will trigger the new behavior or state?"* "When I realize it is time to speak, and I see all those faces turn to look at me expectantly."

4. Congruence ("ecology"). *"How will your desired outcome affect other aspects of your life, either positively or negatively? Does any part of you have any objection to your having this outcome?"* "If I were able to do this, my boss might ask me to do sales presentations at out-of-town conferences, and be away from my family more, which I wouldn't like."

There are three fundamental alternatives for resolving objections arising from competing outcomes:

a. Limit the outcome to the appropriate contexts. Example: "I only want to use this ability in professional contexts involving colleagues, or at presentations for the PTA and other school functions for my kids."
b. Revise the outcome so that conflict no longer occurs. Example: "I only want to be able to give casual conversational talks, which aren't appropriate for larger sales presentations."
c. Teach behavioral competence to deal successfully with the undesired consequences. Example: "I need to learn the ability to politely, respectfully, and firmly refuse my boss's requests to travel more."

5. **Blocks.** *"What stops you from having your desired outcome already?"* "I get nervous, and that makes my hands shake and my voice quaver, and sometimes I forget what I want to say."
6. **Existing resources.** *"What resources do you already have that will support getting your outcome?"* "I feel comfortable speaking to you, and to small groups of friends, where I have no difficulty remembering what I want to say."
7. **Additional resources.** *"What other resources do you need in order to get your outcome?"* "I need to learn how to feel comfortable in larger groups, and I need to learn how to make notes or find some other way to remind me of what I want to say, as a backup in case I lose my train of thought."
8. **Steps.**
    a. Path. *"How are you going to get there?"* "I'll start practicing in very small groups of two or three people, and I'll imagine that they are all close friends."
    b. Alternatives. *"Do you have more than one way to get there?"* (The more alternatives the better.) "I can also start by giving little talks to my kids about dinosaurs, or by presenting accounting figures to the PTA."
    c. Chunking. *"Is the first step specified and achievable? How about subsequent steps?"* "I can sign up for Toastmasters, where there is no risk, and I can begin by giving very short presentations, so that it is easier to remember what I want to say. Then I can make slightly longer presentations, and use file cards with cue words to help me remember."
9. **Meta-outcome.** In this process, whenever you can foresee that your outcome will have troublesome consequences, elicit the outcome of the outcome (a "meta-outcome") by asking, *"What will that outcome do for you?"* or *"What will you get if you do that?"* Keep asking until you get an outcome that you think is

positive and not problematic. Finding a meta-outcome gives you flexibility in finding a specific behavior that will give you what you really want (the meta-outcome) without the drawbacks of the initial outcome that you thought you wanted. Then run this meta-outcome through the outcome specification process. "If I learn how to speak in public, I can spread ideas that will benefit others; I guess if I did that through writing, instead; I might be able to reach more people, and not have to learn to be a good speaker or travel."

This process of specifying an outcome can also be applied to your self-talk. There are some very important conditions that need to be met in order to specify how you can talk to yourself in a useful way. You can examine the words you say internally, to be sure that they get you what you really want, without too many significant undesired costs or consequences. In the next chapter, I explore how you are already talking to yourself, and how to use an extensive checklist to change that into something that will serve you much better, and take you where you want to go in life.

10 Asking Questions

When we ask ourselves a question, it directs our attention to certain aspects of our experience, and ignores others. If I'm at a restaurant, and it is time to order a meal, I could ask myself a wide variety of questions, and each one would point my mind in a different direction. For instance, imagine that you are in a restaurant now, and the waiter or waitress has just handed you the menu. What question do you ask yourself? . . .

First write down your question, and then notice how that question directed your attention, and how you feel as a result of asking it. . . .

We will make use of your question later in this chapter, so if you haven't yet written down your question, pause to do so now, so that you won't miss out on a useful learning. . . .

I realize that it may not yet be clear what I am asking you to do, so I offer you some examples below. Ask yourself the following questions, one at a time, and then pause to notice how each one directs your mind to a different scope of experience, and results in a somewhat different feeling:

1. What food would I enjoy most? . . .
2. What should I order? . . .
3. What are other people ordering? . . .
4. Did I pick a good restaurant? . . .
5. What is least expensive? . . .
6. What food will feel best to me an hour from now? . . .

This is only a very small sample of the many possible questions that someone could ask in this situation. I'll offer some general observations about each one below, and you can compare that with your experience of each.

The first question directs your attention to think of something that will satisfy your own tastes, pleasures, and preferences. Probably you will have a feeling of pleasure, as you imagine tasting the foods that you enjoy most. While choosing a meal that you will enjoy makes a lot of sense, it could result in spending more than you can afford, or in an overindulgence that you may regret later.

The second question uses a different criterion, *should* instead of your own enjoyment. Often this means choosing according to some set of rules about what you should do, which is often different from what you would enjoy. "I'd like a steak, but I should have a salad and juice so I can lose weight." Since most people resist doing what they "should" do, you likely have a less satisfying feeling of being pushed to do something that you'd rather not do.

The third question directs your attention to what other people are ordering, rather than what would satisfy you. If you select a meal based on what others select, and they enjoy different kinds of food than you do, you may choose a meal that you don't enjoy, and might even dislike intensely.

The fourth question directs your attention to the overall quality of the food at this restaurant. Whether you decide that the food is likely to be good, bad, or indifferent, that is irrelevant to deciding which food to choose. However, this would be a good question to ask earlier in time, when you are deciding on a restaurant, or it might be useful if you are thinking that perhaps you made a poor choice, and you are considering moving to a different restaurant.

The fifth question directs your attention to the price, rather than to the food. While this may be a good choice if you have little money to spend, it will restrict your choices and sometimes will result in ordering something that is not enjoyable. You may feel some regret that you can't order the food that you would choose if you had more money to spend.

The sixth question directs your attention to a future feeling of the food in your stomach—a pleasant feeling of fullness or lightness—rather than the pleasure of tasting the food. You may choose a meal that isn't quite as pleasurable, but you will probably seldom overindulge or become overweight.

If you review your experience of these questions, you will find that each one offers certain benefits and each one also has certain drawbacks, which will be true of any question that you could ask. Depending on the context, and your outcome at the moment, any of them could be useful, but each of them will also have certain disadvantages.

You may also discover that one or more of these questions seems very familiar or logical ("Oh, yeah, that makes sense") while others seem alien or nonsensical ("I'd never ask that!"). That kind of response indicates that you would typically tend to ask one kind of question, rather than another.

Now return to the question that you first asked yourself at the beginning of this chapter. Find out what you can discover about how it directs your attention, your feeling as a result, and what the potential benefits and drawbacks of this question are. . . .

Core Question

Originally developed by Leslie LeBeau and called the "Virtual Question," I have adapted her method here, calling it the "core question." A core question is a fundamental question that each of us continually asks throughout the day, unconsciously organizing and directing our experience in ways that can be both enabling and limiting—a powerful determinant of our skills, attitudes, and abilities. When you discover your core question, that gives you an opportunity to examine it for its advantages and limitations, and change it to something more useful to you.

Since this question is one that we typically ask, regardless of the context, it is so familiar that we tend to presuppose it and take it for granted, just as the fish takes water for granted. It is so much a part of who we are that it is unconscious, so it is difficult to identify what it is. The first step in this process is to become even more familiar with the impact of different questions. The instructions below are written as an exercise to do with two other people, because you can learn so much by comparing what you do with what someone else does. But you can also do the exercise by yourself. Another way to gain a wider experience is to then take a friend through the exercise, and notice how different some of his or her answers are.

1. Introduction: Experimenting With Examples

Think of a context that is important to you that involves at least one other person. Keeping that context the same, experiment with several of the questions below, in order to discover how different questions alter your experience. Notice how your experience of the same event changes when you ask each question internally. Particularly notice how the scope of your attention shifts, and also any shifts in the three major sensory modalities—visual images, auditory sounds, and kinesthetic feelings.

What can I get here?
What do you want?
Aren't I clever?
What should I do?
Am I safe?
Do I have a place here?
What's wrong?
What do they want from me?
Have I done everything I could have?
Am I included?
How does it work?
What is my place here?
Am I well?
How else could it be?
Do I want this?
How am I doing?
What's most important?
What do I have to contribute?
Am I good enough?
Is this all there is?
Who's in charge?
How can I help?

Do they love me?

Is it right?

What's happening to me?

If I survive this, what's next?

Do I belong?

How can this give me pleasure?

Will I survive this?

Am I being understood?

How could this be better?

What's missing?

What should I do next?

How can I make the most of this situation?

I hope it is obvious to you how different questions create very different worlds of experience. "Do I belong?" can easily result in feelings of being abandoned, "Will I survive this?" in feelings of desperation, and "How can I make the most of this situation?" in feelings of optimism and empowerment.

Pause to share your experience of a number of these questions with at least one other person, compare what you noticed with what others noticed, and discuss what kind of personal world each one creates. . . .

2. Select a Context

Now think of an example of an important context in your life: home, work, relationship, children, and so on, that includes at least one other person. Notice how you represent this example in all three major modalities (images, sounds, and feelings). Also notice the submodalities of your experience—the smaller elements within each modality, such as the brightness, size, color, distance, motion or stillness, or depth or flatness of the visual image, the loudness, tonality, and tempo of any auditory words or sounds, and the intensity, extent, and qualities—hardness, temperature, and so on—of any tactile kinesthetic feelings you have. . . .

3. Eliciting Your Core Question

Method 1

While thinking of your experience of this major life context, ask yourself, "If there were a question, always in the back of my mind, that quietly guided all my experience and behavior in this context, what might it be?" Imagine that this question is just underneath your conscious awareness, directing your attention, and guiding all your perceptions and behavior.

Write this question down, and then think of your important life context again, and imagine asking this question there. If this question changes your representation of this context, it's probably not quite the right one. Your core question will fit the context so well that it won't change your representation when you ask it. Try adjusting your question until you find one that fits better. . . .

Now think of the opposite of your core question—whatever opposite means to you. Write this question down, and then notice how it changes your experience of the same example of the important life context when you imagine asking it. . . .

Experimenting with the opposite of your question offers a vivid contrast for realizing the impact of a question, and it often clarifies what your question might be. You can also try the alternate method below for eliciting your core question.

Method 2

Think of a profoundly altered state you have experienced that was pleasant. It doesn't matter whether this state happened spontaneously or was induced by a meditation practice or a drug. . . .

Put yourself back into this state, experience it, and identify what makes it strikingly different from your usual experience. In an altered state the core question is either not asked or is completely answered, and this is one of the factors that makes this state altered. This altered state will be the opposite of your usual state.

For example, one man said, "When I was in that state I thought, 'What are people afraid of?' I was amazed that people could be scared of anything. I felt completely safe." This indicates a core question about safety that might be something like, "Am I safe?" or "How safe am I?" Since he usually continually focused on safety, being completely safe and not needing to test for safety was a very altered state for him. Another person said, "In that state it was very clear that there was nothing to be done; everything was perfect as it was." The opposite of this might be something like "What shall I do next?" or "What needs to be done?"

Using these understandings, determine what is different about your altered state. . . .

Then think of a core question that is the opposite of your experience in the altered state. . . .

4. Try Out Your Core Question

Try your question in some other major life contexts to see how well it fits there. Make any adjustments that you can think of to make it fit better in all those different contexts. For instance, "What food shall I choose?" would be limited to only a few contexts, but "What should I do next?" is more general, so it could be used for choosing food, as well as anywhere else that you need to make a decision.

5. Share Your Experiences

Share what you found in steps 3 and 4 with the other people you are doing the exercise with, in order to get a broader range of experience with the impact of different questions. . . .

6. Experimenting and Adjusting

Next, try on the questions of the others in your group, one at a time. Notice how these different questions change your experience. When you try on these different core questions, what aspects do you like, dislike, find interesting or useful, and so on? . . .

Again, share your experience with the others in your trio. . . .

7. Examine a Question

As a trio, choose a core question that one of you discovered and examine it, using the checklist below, to identify possible problems or limitations. Keep in mind that a core question is a very condensed distillation that is embedded in all of a person's presuppositions, beliefs, and ways of organizing his or her experience. Also keep in mind that each word in a core question can have quite different meanings to different people. A question that works well for one person may work very differently for someone else. The checklist is only a way to alert you to possible limitations that you might not otherwise notice, and they can be a focus for experimenting with modifications or alternatives in the next step of this exercise.

Checklist

Note that items are not listed in order of importance or any other hierarchy.

a. **What is presupposed?** Negate the question and notice what is still true. An effective core question presupposes choice, ability, resources, good feelings, and so on.
b. **What modal operator(s) are contained in the question?** Modal operators are words that indicate possibility, choice, desire, or necessity—and their negations. A useful core question will usually include possibility, choice, and desire, and not necessity or negations of possibility, choice, or desire (Andreas, 2006).
c. **What verb tense is used?** For example, past, present, future, conditional, subjunctive. Since the past can't be changed, a question directing attention to the present and future will usually be more useful in enabling choice, ability, and satisfaction.
d. **Self/other emphasis or sorting.** Notice pronouns: I, you, they, we, and so on. Ideally there is a balance between attending to self and others, with respect and consideration for both.

e. **Active or passive.** Is the person the active subject or passive object of the question? For instance, "What shall I do?" is active and empowering, while "What will happen to me?" is passive, and presupposes lack of choice.
f. **Is there a negation?** For example, "What's wrong" means "not right." Try transforming any negations into positive statements. For instance, "What's wrong" could become, "How can I make this better?" "What do I want to attend to?" or "What can I learn from this?"
g. **Are there any comparisons?** For example, more, less, better, best, enough, and so on. Is there a comparison of self and other, self and self, or other and other? Does a comparison offer useful feedback information, and result in useful feelings of pleasure and motivation? Try changing or eliminating the comparison.
h. **Is it a yes/no (digital) question, or an analog continuum?** "Am I safe?" is a digital or binary question with only two possible answers, while "How safe am I?" is an analog (continuum) question with much more choice. Usually analog questions will be more useful.
i. **Is it a spurious yes/no question?** Is it stated so that it can only be answered in one way? For instance, "Did I do everything I could have?" or "Am I completely safe?" can never be answered "yes" in a complex and changing world.
j. **Sensory-based.** Does the question direct the person's attention toward specific sensory-based events and behaviors? For instance, "What's happening around me right now?" directs attention to specific external events, but "Am I safe?" doesn't.
k. **Note any cause and effect** ("this caused that"), **equivalence** ("this equals that"), or **context** that is stated, referred to, or presupposed. These are the three structures of meaning (Andreas, 2006).
l. Which of the three major aspects of experience—**behavior, thinking,** and **feeling**—are included, omitted, or presupposed?
m. **Does it contain a self-reflexive loop?** "How well am I doing?" in contrast to "How well did that work?" Usually self-reflexive loops are not useful, because they isolate you from your surroundings.
n. **Does the question elicit motivation** that is "toward," "away from," or both? Experiment with changing this orientation.
o. **Are the feelings that result from the question pleasant, unpleasant, or neither?** How could you change the question to make the resulting feelings more positive?

8. Experiment With Modifications or Adjustments

As a trio, suggest changes in the wording of the question. The person whose question it is can try out each change, one at a time, to see if he or she likes the modification.

For instance, if the original question was "Am I loved?" that is passive and a yes/no (digital) question. You could try, "What can I do to be sure she loves me?" which is more active. Or you could try, "How much am I loved?" which presupposes that you are loved; it is just a matter of how much. Or you could combine the two changes in a question like, "What can I do to make her love me more?" As the person whose question it is tries out a modification, be particularly attentive to their nonverbal responses, which will indicate how well it does or doesn't fit for them. The person with the question is the only judge of whether any such modification fits better for them. Make a note of changes that the person likes better. . . .

9. Congruence Check ("Ecology")

Whenever you find a change that you like, and that you think you would like to have as part of your automatic unconscious responding, test it thoroughly by imagining asking the question in all your major life contexts, being alert for any possible problems, limitations, or complications. If you notice problems, experiment to find out how you can adjust the question so that these problems don't arise. . . .

10. Rehearse in Future Contexts

Assuming that you have identified one or more changes that you are congruently pleased with, rehearse the modified question in a variety of future situations, so that the question will generalize widely and become a spontaneous unconscious response.

11. Testing and Feedback

Make a promise to yourself to check a week or two in the future to find out how well these changes are working for you. You can always make further modifications any time you want to.

You can take any problem situation, find out what question you are asking there, and then modify it to lead your attention in a more satisfying direction. When you change a core question, that change will usually generalize far beyond the problem situation that you began with. Accordingly, it is really important to carefully test any changes in a variety of major life contexts, to be sure that it functions well in all of them. (A live workshop presentation of this process is available on CD at www.realpeoplepress.com, Andreas, S., *Core Questions*, Milton Erickson Foundation conference, "Brief Therapy, Lasting Impressions," December 2006.)

Next we will learn how to combine a number of the methods you have learned into a playful and enjoyable intervention.

11 Transforming a Message

In previous chapters we have experimented with a wide variety of ways to change the impact of a troublesome negative voice. Next I want to offer you a way of using several of these different elements together so that they all support each other in creating an even more powerful change intervention. This new method below was developed recently by Melanie Davis, a therapist in the UK. Besides being effective, it is also playful and enjoyable. As you read about it, and the examples that Melanie gives, I encourage you to notice the different elements in it.

Inner Resolving

> I have been working with people who are recovering from drug and/or alcohol addiction on a daily basis during the last 3 years in an EU-funded project which helped people who were long term unemployed get back into work or training opportunities. I began to realize very quickly that it was mostly the way that they were saying things to themselves internally—often without being aware of it—that was the major cause of their problems. The things that they say on the inside easily talk themselves into a variety of unpleasant feelings, including depression, anxiety, and fear, and this usually intensifies their addiction.
>
> One woman shared with me her daily thought that repeated without a break from the moment she woke in the morning until she went to sleep at night: "I don't know whether I am good enough, I don't know whether I am good enough, I don't know whether I am good enough. . . ." Another woman told me that she kept hearing herself say, "I'm no good, I'm no good, I'm no good. . . ."
>
> A young girl who was totally lost and alone and feeling suicidal was repeating, "Nobody needs me to be around. . . ."
>
> A man who had been in prison for a long time, suffering from depression, and struggling with coming off drugs, was repeating to himself, "I'm useless. . . ."
>
> One wonderful lady hadn't slept through the night for as long as she could remember. When asked what she was telling herself, she said she repeated over and over, "Don't think I will sleep tonight. . . ."
>
> I have worked with over 500 clients in the past 3 years and the examples above are quite typical. This got me to wondering, and I had the thought, "With so many people saying all these things to themselves, they couldn't be all wrong." Maybe they were right, but the messages had been misunderstood.
>
> So with the woman who told me she kept hearing herself saying, "I don't know whether I am good enough," I found myself doing something very different.
>
> First, I had her write the sentence down on a large piece of paper, and say it out loud to me with the same intonation and inflection. As you can imagine, it really didn't sound very nice.
>
> Next I changed two things:

One was using phonological ambiguity to change "whether" to "weather."

The other was a full stop (period) after the word "weather" so that it became, "I don't know weather."

Then I asked her to breathe in and wonder if it mattered that she didn't know weather, when there were plenty of people who did, so she could always find out if she needed to know weather.

At this point she started laughing and told me that every morning when she was seated at the breakfast table, one of the women that she lived with would sit down next to her and tell her all about the weather in Scotland for that day, whether she had asked her to or not. This might have been really useful, except for the fact that she lived in Wales!

I had her repeat the sentence, "I don't know weather," and then had her add a little bit extra, "But it's OK, because Janice does," which made her laugh uncontrollably.

When her laughter subsided, I said, "Now say the rest of the sentence." She took a breath in and said, "I am good enough." To her surprise, she took another deep breath and sighed, smiled, and repeated the words, "I am good enough." "Nice," I said, "that's what you've been telling yourself for a long time now," to which she sighed, and then burst out laughing again.

The next morning she met me by the front door and said, "This morning when I woke up, I looked in the mirror and said, 'I am good enough.' Then I rushed downstairs to find out if it was snowing in Scotland!"

This day was a real catalyst for me; I began to wonder "weather" this was going to be the beginning of something really exciting!

During my group confidence session that morning I began to play around with other clients' internal dialogue. When one of the women said, "I'm no good," I smiled and asked her if she would be willing to tune in to what she was really saying. She looked intrigued and said, "Sure, go ahead; I have felt like I am no good forever."

I divided the sentence into two parts, and wrote the first part on the board, "I am" (which is only a different way of writing "I'm") and had her repeat it and know that it was an undeniable statement: "I am." "Yes, you are," I told her. Then I had her repeat "I am" to herself until she began smiling.

Then I changed the second part of her original sentence from "no good" to "know good." "Yes, you do," I said, "and I think it's more of a command, something you are supposed to do. So what good do you know?" She smiled and began listing good things that she knew. The whole group joined in and began helping her list good things, until it became a "good things" session. That afternoon she applied for a job at the local college, and she told me it was the first job she had applied for in several years.

One young woman I worked with recently had been suicidal on more than one occasion. When I asked her what she told herself she said, "Nobody needs me to be around."

I wrote the first part of her sentence out for her so it looked like this: "Know body." She literally gasped as she read the words and told me that she struggled with eating, and had never really liked her body. I asked her what would be different if she really knew her body. She smiled, and said, "I would probably eat something and feel good."

Then I wrote the next part of her sentence, "needs me to be around," and asked her, "Who?" She began to cry through a deep smile, and listed all the people in her life who needed her to be around.

Now take a minute or two to think how you could apply this process to the man who felt really depressed and useless as he was coming off drugs, repeatedly telling himself the sentence, "I'm useless." . . .

I told him that this was actually a really good suggestion that he was giving himself, to which he looked somewhat puzzled. I wrote "I am," and had him repeat this statement to himself, as I kept telling him, "Yes, you are."

Then in a command tone, I took the last word and said, "Use less! Use less! Use less!" At this point he started laughing. I am really happy to say that 6 months after the session he is completely free from drugs.

Now pause again, to think how you might use this method with the adorable lady who was sent to me by her general practitioner suffering from severe insomnia, who said to herself, "Don't think I will sleep tonight. . . ." She said that the dialogue was really fast and harsh and she lay awake listening to it every night for hours on end. . . .

I suggested to her that her internal dialogue was something like a small child that was being ignored; the more it was ignored, the louder and faster it became. I asked her if she had ever wondered if she might be giving herself some really good advice, and she shook her head. When she asked me to explain, I wrote this for her: "Don't think!" and said to her, "Breathe in, and wonder what it would be like to not think." She smiled, and I followed up with, "And when you don't think, what do you think will happen?" She smiled really broadly, and said, "I will sleep tonight." And she did.

By using this method I have found a very gentle, enjoyable, and playful way of teaching clients to tune in to the good things that they have been trying to tell themselves. The result of this exploration has been a total transformation in the way I work with people. I now teach this as part of my confidence workshops as well as using it in one-to-one therapy. (Davis, personal communication 2010)

Elements of the Method

1. Presuppose that what your client has been saying to himself is positive and useful, but has been badly misunderstood.

2. Divide the sentence into two or more parts. We have learned to divide the flow of language into words and phrases in conventional ways, but we can also learn to divide it in new and different ways.
3. Use auditory ambiguity to find a different meaning in the same sounds (or similar sounds) that is more positive, enjoyable, humorous, or even nonsensical.
4. Use a different intonation and inflection that is cheerful, playful, and humorous, instead of the serious or unpleasant one in the original statement. Using a tone that indicates a question, exclamation, or command can often be helpful.
5. The meaning of the message is changed, but no attempt is made to change the intensity of the client's feeling response. This is a key factor that can easily be overlooked. Since the client has been responding to the voice's old message very intensely, she will respond equally strongly to the new message, and this will be augmented by her surprise at the new meaning. Many of the methods in this book reduce the intensity of response to a voice, but in this case we leave that intact, making sure their new response is also intense.

The presupposition that the client has actually been saying something positive to herself for so long changes the meaning of the whole utterance. Changing the punctuation of the sentence changes the scope of what is attended to, which often automatically changes the meaning of the resulting smaller pieces. Finding an auditory ambiguity changes how that set of sounds is categorized, which changes the meaning. Using a playful and creative tonality and adding other tonal shifts that indicate a question, exclamation, or command changes the music that carries the words, also changing the meaning. When these four elements are joined together in one intervention, they all support each other in changing the meaning and feeling response to that new meaning.

When someone is disturbed by what he is saying to himself, he has only one meaning for that set of words, and he has no choice about how to interpret that series of sounds. Melanie's process creates a new meaning for the same set of sounds. Previously they had only one meaning; now they have two—or sometimes more than two. The old meaning was unpleasant, and the new one is much more enjoyable. So it makes sense to choose the one that is more pleasant, and the old unpleasant meaning tends to recede into the background of attention. If you offer a third (or fourth) meaning for the same set of words, the client has even more choice in how to respond. Usually when we say the word *choice*, we use the word in a vague way that only means, "You could do something different," without saying what that might be, or how to do it. This process offers specific alternative meanings, providing a real basis for choice.

Despite Melanie's wonderful examples, when I first tried using this method, I found that it was a lot more difficult than I expected. I found it very hard to set aside the usual meaning of the words and just listen to the sounds to find other words with different meanings—it was a real stretch of my flexibility and creativity. In order to practice this more, I asked a colleague who specializes in insomnia to tell me what some of his clients said to themselves that kept them awake. In the following exercise, you will find a number of these sentences, which you can use to practice with.

Inner Resolving Exercise

Use Melanie's method with each of the sentences below. If you can do this with three or four other people, working as a group, you will all benefit from each other's inventiveness. If the group gets stuck on one sentence, just go on to try the next one. Later, when you return to one that you got stuck on, you may find that your subconscious mind has continued to work on it, and that you now notice other possibilities.

1. "I'll never be able to sleep."
2. "I'll always have trouble sleeping."
3. "I'm worried I'll never sleep again."
4. "I'm afraid I won't be able to sleep."
5. "I can't sleep."
6. "Sleep is difficult."
7. "Something's wrong with me."

When I tried this exercise, I still found it difficult to do, so I sent these examples to Melanie and asked her to tell me what she would do with them. The following is what she sent me in return:

1. For this sentence I might try humor: "I'll never be a bull" (phonetic pronunciation, full stop, playing with this concept, smiling, laughing). Next part of the sentence: "To sleep" (said softly with a command down tone, adding some "shhh" noises).
2. I would take it like this: "I'll" becomes "I will," using command tone down as in "This is my will." Then add "All ways"; "I will all ways"—playing around with the concept of willing all ways. Then add "have," becoming "I will all ways have." Then "trouble" becomes "treble" (using a French or European accent can be more than helpful here) to yield, "Treble sleeping" (times three sleeping). Then repeat softly, "One sleeping, two sleeping, treble sleeping . . ." until the sounds become like the counting down into sleep stage by stage, softer and softer. "One sleeping, double sleeping, treble sleeping . . . I will all ways have treble sleeping."

3. "I am." Full stop, and explore the concept of "I am"—a person, clever, determined, resourceful, problem solver, beautiful, and so on. "Worried? I will (my will) never!" So the sentence becomes "I am. I will worry?" (Rhetorical question.) "Never!" as I am resourceful, determined, problem solver, and so on. Full stop, deep breath, pause . . . followed by "sleep again" (command tone down, softly).
4. "I am" (a person, strong, survivor, funny, determined, resourceful, problem solver, beautiful, etc.). "Afraid?" (Rhetorical question.) "I won't" becomes "I will not" (because I am—a person, strong, survivor, funny, determined, resourceful, problem solver, beautiful, etc.) "be a bull"—"I will not be a bull!" (humor, laughter, and pause here). "To sleep." (Shhhh, now.) Or with a full stop after "I will not," the end of the sentence becomes, "Be able to sleep." (Shhhh, now.)
5. First change "I can't" to "I can not" (full stop). Then to, "I can knot" (really helpful when tying shoe laces—giggle and smiles). "Sleep" (Command tone down, shhh . . .).
6. "Sleep is?" (Add question mark, and—hmm) "difficult" to define. Let's explore a bit. (What kind of cult is it?)
7. "Some thing is wrong." "Sum thing is wrong." (Full stop, how am I adding things up wrong?) "With me" (add "Who is?"—my partner, children, dog, etc.). (M. Davis, personal communication, 2010)

When I presented this exercise in a seminar, participants came up with additional new meanings for the sentences above, some of which are presented below. Before reading on, back up to the list of problem sentences above, and see if you can come up with alternatives. Then when you read the sentences below, play with different intonations, pauses, accents, and so on, and find out how many variations you can create with the same new set of words. . . .

1. "I'll never! Be able to sleep."
   "I will?—Never! . . . Be able! . . . To sleep."
2. "I WILL all ways! Have tray bowl sleeping."
3. "I'm worried?—I'll never! . . . Sleep again."
   "I'm worried I'll never schlep again."
4. "I'm afraid I won. . . . T'be able to sleep."
   "I'm afraid I won't be a bowl. . . . To sleep."
   "I'm a frayed! . . . I won't be a bowl. . . . To sleep."
5. "I can! . . . T'sleep."
   "Eye can? . . . T'sleep."
   "Icon knots leap."
   "I can knot! . . . Sleep."
   "I can't? . . . Sleep."
6. "Sleep is. . . . Defy cult." (Or "Daffy cult.")
7. "Something is. . . . Row on with me."

"Some thin sarong with me."
"So! Me thing is wrong with me."
"Some think strong with me."

Second Exercise

The next step in your learning is to do the same kind of intervention with additional examples. It can be particularly helpful to find three or four colleagues or friends and do this in a playful brainstorming group, in which you can benefit from each other's creativity and flexibility. Think about what you say to yourself that troubles you, and/or think of what your clients say to themselves that interferes with their happiness, and write them all down. Then each person in the group can offer one of these sentences. If you do this without saying whether it is your own sentence, or a client's, that protects your privacy. Then the group can find new positive, playful, or ridiculous meanings in what that voice is saying. You can start with Melanie's format, and then add in other elements that you have explored in earlier chapters. For instance, you could sing the new message, or change the volume as if it were moving nearer and then farther away, or moving from right to left in front of you, and so on.

If you do this exercise with some friends, I can assure you of two things: (1) there will be lots and lots of laughter, and (2) whether or not your clients benefit, you will increase your own flexibility and creativity immeasurably, and the effects of this will radiate far beyond this specific method, and permeate everything you do. Here are some examples from a recent seminar to practice with if you can't easily meet with others to practice doing this.

1. "It's just so awful!"
2. "I'm so inadequate."
3. "Why can't I get this done?"
4. "What if it doesn't work?"
5. "It's not fair."
6. "I'm not worthy."
7. "No one likes me."
8. "I'm not good enough."

Please pause here to play with each of the sentences above before reading on to see what others did with them.

Below are a number of examples that seminar participants came up with for the list of sentences above. Try each one with different intonation, emphasis, and accent, and notice how much changes as a result of changing the tone to indicate exclamation, question, or command.

1. "It is. . . . Just so. . . . Awe full." (Or "Ahhhh, full.")
2. "I'm so IN! Adequate?"

3. "Why can't I? . . . Get this DONE!"
4. "What if?—It doesn't work! (Referring to the "what if.")
5. "It is! Not fair?
   "It's not fare!" (Food to eat.)
   "It's a nut fair."
   "It's a knot fair." (Italian accent)
6. "I'm noteworthy."
   "I am!—Not worthy?"
7. "No! ONE likes me."
   "Know: one likes me!"
8. "I'm naughty! Good enough?"
   "I AM! Not good enough?"
   "I'm no T. Good enough."
   "I know, 'tis good enough."

Summary

In previous chapters we have thoroughly explored how to change one element of a troubling voice at a time, in order to discover how to change its meaning. We first experimented with changing the location, tempo, and tonality of a voice. Next we discovered the usefulness of adding music, a song, or additional voices. We have experimented with changing *I* to *you*, and how to create an affirmation skillfully so that it doesn't boomerang with negative results and make things worse. We also explored how to start the day with several other more useful ways to talk to ourselves. We have clarified the dangers in how we generalize, evaluate, presuppose, and delete, so that we can avoid these common linguistic traps. We have learned how to avoid the unpleasant pitfalls of negations by transforming "nots" into statements of positive outcomes, so that we can more easily have the kinds of experiences we want to have. And we have explored how to ask ourselves useful questions, focusing on what will enable us to have the kinds of experiences that will be effective, satisfying, and empowering. In this last chapter we have learned how to change the punctuation and music of a sentence in order to give it a completely different meaning.

When people begin to learn how to sing or play a musical instrument, they spend a lot of time with scales, or with very simple pieces of music, in order to learn what their voice or instrument can do, and how to control it to produce the sounds they want. With further practice, they move on to sing or play longer and more complex pieces. The skills they learn by doing this can eventually become the foundation for creative improvisation, in which they spontaneously create new sequences and combinations of sounds. You did the same thing when you first learned to use language. As an infant, you began by using single sounds to indicate something or get what you wanted: "Wawa!" "Gimme." "Yight." "Ish."

Then you learned to put two words together into what is called *pivot grammar*: "Me go." "Goggie bark." "Baby poopy."

Then gradually you learned to put even more words together into much longer and more complex sentences, along with the tonal and tempo shifts that supported what you wanted to communicate. All your life you have continued to develop your use of language. This book is really only a continuation of that process, directing your attention to elements of language that you may have been unaware of, or only vaguely aware of, in order to give you more options and empowering choices in your life.

The particular combination of elements in Melanie's method is only one of many possibilities. By presenting it in a format in which you can learn it easily, like a simple song or piece of music, you can gain competence and fluency. When you have practiced all of the different elements in this book thoroughly, they can become second nature. That creates a foundation for spontaneous improvisation, and you will find yourself using them in all sorts of combinations, depending on what someone presents you with.

For instance, I recently worked with a woman who had been told by her doctor that she had a serious disease, and that she had "2 months to 6 years to live" in a doom-and-gloom tone of voice. She thought of this as a very serious "death sentence," and was very angry with the doctor, both for what he said and the way that he said it. This memory had terrorized her during the 2 years since then.

One of the first things I did was to laugh heartily and say something like, "Doctors and their predictions! Do you know what I do when a doctor makes a prediction like that? . . . I look around at all the walls [I elaborately pantomimed craning my neck to look around at all the walls of the office, looking for diplomas] and then I look at the doctor [I turned and looked directly into her eyes, which directed the message—apparently directed to the doctor—to the woman as well] and ask, 'Do you have a fortune-telling license?'" This—and my supporting laughter, attitude, and nonverbal expression—changed the meaning of the "death sentence" to "fortune-telling," which is much more doubtful, and she laughed along with me.

Then I asked her to close her eyes and imagine a conversation with the doctor in which she told him about her anger, and expressed anything else that she wanted to say to him. As she did this, she was the dominant person in the conversation, speaking forcefully while the doctor listened passively. This empowered her and reduced the power of what the doctor had said, reducing the traumatic impact of the memory. When she was done, she smiled and said that she could now breathe more easily.

A bit later, I said to her, "Just now you were able to 'diss' your doctor with ease, . . . so you really do have 'diss' ease!"—

completely changing the meaning of the word *disease* and her response to it. She laughed freely, and felt even more relief.

The elements of language that we have explored together in this book create a basis for very rapid and easy change that can have profound results in bettering your client's lives—and also your own. Enjoy.